EYE

of the

BEAST

THE TRUE STORY OF
SERIAL KILLER JAMES WOOD

Terry Adams
Mary Brooks-Mueller, Scott Shaw

Addicus Books, Inc. Om

An Addicus Nonfiction Book

ISBN 1-886039-32-1

Cover design by George Foster, Jeff Reiner
Typography by Linda Dageforde

Library of Congress Cataloging-in-Publication Data

Adams, Terry, 1946-
    Eye of the beast : the true story of serial killer James Wood / Terry Adams, Scott Shaw, Mary Brooks-Mueller.
        p.   cm.
    ISBN 1-886039-32-1 (alk. paper)
    1. Wood, James, 1947- . 2. Serial murders—Idaho—Case studies.
    I. Shaw, Scott, 1953-   . II. Brooks-Mueller, Mary, 1954-
    III. Title.
    HV6533.U8A33 1997   97-34332
    364.15'23'0978647—dc21   CIP

Addicus Books, Inc.
P.O. Box 45327
Omaha, Nebraska 68145
Web site: http://members.aol.com/addicusbks

Printed in the United States of America
10 9 8 7 6 5 4 3 2 1

To the memory of Jeralee

Authors' Notes

James Wood is not like other serial killers. He has no victim preference, no sexual preference. He is opportunistic and will abuse, assault, rape, kill, or mutilate anybody, anytime. The social standards that motivate most of us to abide by the law and lead lives of decency are the very triggers for Wood to lie, steal, and murder.

Upon his arrest, he told Detective Scott Shaw, "I'm a monster. I have demons inside of me." Later, he told Mary Brooks-Mueller, "I'll write you from prison and pour my heart out to you. Maybe you can unscramble it."

In reality, James Wood has no conscience. He is not possessed by demons, but rather by rage and vengeance. He lives to manipulate, control, and deceive. Yet he looks quite ordinary. He is a master at pretending to be normal. You wouldn't notice him in a crowd. But make no mistake, he is a predator, a career killer.

To assemble this book, we drew in part from our own interviews with James Wood—one of the most unique and dangerous criminals we have encountered in our two decades of law enforcement work. In all, we spent four years researching Wood and his crimes. We interviewed dozens of individuals. Some of their names have been changed to protect their privacy. We pored over thousands of pages of court documents, mental evaluations, and forensic records to tell this story.

We hope this book will help educate readers about the true nature of the psychopath and, in turn, help protect others from the likes of James Wood.

Prologue

August 1993. Bannock County Jail. Pocatello, Idaho. "Tell me about the two girls in Shreveport," Detective Scott Shaw asked. "The ones in 1967."

"Scott, I tell you, I was so drunk, it's all just a blur." James Wood said, leaning back in his chair. He took a deep drag off his cigarette and thumped the ashes down the floor drain. "They were just whores, anyway. Maybe the devil just wanted it to happen, and he chose me to carry out his work."

"Jim, do you know what *manipulative mitigation* is?" Shaw asked.

"Can't say as I do."

"It's self-serving bullshit. It means you have an excuse for everything you do. You were drunk or the devil wanted you to do it. You'll say anything you can think of to get yourself off the hook, and when you think I've bought into it, you start with the 'I've found God' stuff. I don't buy it Jim. You think you're playing games with me, that you can control me. I'm not a little girl who doesn't have a clue about dealing with some-body like you. You're wasting my time."

"You're saying I'm evil?"

"No, I'm saying you're full of crap. I know you're used to dealing with people and situations you can control. I'm saying, drop the 'poor pitiful me' garbage and get to the point. You're starting to piss me off."

Shaw saw Wood's anger starting to surface. Wood leaned forward in his chair and glared at the detective. "So, what is it you want to know, Scott?"

"Tell me about the two girls in Shreveport."

"They were just two bitches I met in a bar. I had just got me a Pontiac GTO. One night it got stolen. I was so pissed, I couldn't fuckin' walk straight. I knew those two girls had something to do with it."

"What made you think they had any anything to do with it?"

"I just figured they did, and the more I thought about it, the madder I got. So I decided to make them pay in a big way. I went to their apartment and told them I was drunk and asked if I could stay 'til I could sober up and go home. When they were asleep, I went to the kitchen and got a knife from one of those things that holds about six knives."

"A wooden knife block?"

"Yeah. Then I went to the bedroom and didn't say anything. I just cut their goddamned throats. I left them there and went back to the kitchen and fixed myself something to eat. I was hungry as hell. After a while, I went back to the bedroom. I figured they were both dead because neither one of them was moving, and there was blood all over the bed. I thought I'd show the bitches, so I drug one out to the dining room. Some way she ended up under the table, and I just screwed her right there. Got blood all over me and everything else."

"You thought she was dead when you raped her?"

"I sure did. But, sonofabitch, I had blood all over me!"

"Why would you want to have sex with a dead person, Jim?"

"Because I showed them not to fuck with me."

"Bullshit. I think sex with a body is just your ultimate form of control. There's no way they can criticize your performance. It seems to me you had what you consider a perfect partner."

"Well, I ain't really sure," Wood said, looking into the eyes of the detective. "But, I'll tell you this...it's the best. She got what she deserved, and I got what I wanted. And I'll tell you something else, Scott. It shocked the shit out of me when I found out them two gals lived." Wood paused, then continued. "And you know, when I got out of prison, I looked one of 'em up. Turned out she was teaching at one of them universities in Florida. I went down there and went right in her class, just to let her see me. That was something!"

"Why would you do that?"

"Just to let the bitch know I was out," Wood said, taking a drag from his cigarette and thumping ashes down the drain. "And to show that I can do any damn thing I want to!"

And this also...has been one of the
dark places of the earth.

Joseph Conrad
Heart of Darkness

1

*S*unday, *October 25, 1992. Near Alton, Illinois.* James Edward Wood was on the run. This time, his fourteen-year-old stepdaughter had "caused" the problem. *It was her own fault, dammit! She shouldn't have been wearin' them skimpy clothes around the house. I told her to change, but she wouldn't mind! It was her own fault!*

Wood took his eyes off the road long enough to look over at his sullen passenger. She was leaning against the door, her head swaying lazily with the movement of the truck, the wind from the open windows swirling her disheveled hair around her face.

As the dark-brown pickup slipped along the empty highway, the night before came back into hazy focus. *Started drinking pretty early in the morning with that ol' boy I spent the night with at the Holiday Inn in St. Louis. Later that afternoon, after he passed out, I drove over the river to Illinois. Met the gal in a biker bar in Alton. Had a few beers, then we went bar-hopping. Let her drive my truck for a while, but she kept popping the clutch. Then we got to that last bar. Must've had close to eighty dollars in my pocket when we went in. Ordered a round for everybody at the bar, but when it came time to pay, I couldn't find my money. The bitch must've taken it! She'd been talking about travelin' out west with me, too. Told me she had a court appearance next week, and said they was probably gonna lock her up, asked if she could travel with me. By God, she had to be the one that took my money. Nobody else got close enough to get it! Her dirty little trick almost caused some serious trouble, too.*

Those two bikers followed us out of the bar after I couldn't pay. But they backed off pretty quickly when I told them, "If you ever want to see the inside of that bar again, just turn around and go right back in." Meant what I said, too, every word of it. Had my finger on the trigger. Didn't even have to show it. Just kept it in my pocket. "Don't crowd me, man, I mean it, don't crowd me!"

Then what? Passed out in the truck, right there on the main street of Alton, Illinois. Slept there in the truck all night. I know the bitch took my money! But I made her pay this morning, by God. Just turned off on that little road and stopped the truck right there in the middle of some farmer's field. "I want my money," I say, and she says she ain't got my money. So I just say, "Well then, if you ain't going to give it up, by God, I'm gonna take it out in screw. You mess with me, bitch, and I'm gonna mess with you." She wanted to hold off, kept asking why we didn't wait 'til we got to a motel room, it's better there in a bed. But I say, "Hell, no, I ain't waiting." And I didn't wait, either, by God. I did it right there on the seat!

They sped along the highway, the sun, now a little higher, filtered through the leaves of the big oak trees lining the road. The woman, hard-looking for her late twenties, had one long tattoo on her arm.

Wood couldn't stop thinking about the eighty dollars. "I want my fucking money, bitch!" Wood shouted, grabbing the woman's arm.

"I already told you, man," she said, snatching her arm away. "I didn't take your fucking money!"

"I had close to eighty dollars in my pocket when we got to that last place," Wood said, gearing down as they came to a traffic signal. "I didn't spend it, and you're the only one who had a chance to take it."

"Look, dude," she said angrily. "I don't know what your problem is, but for the last time, I ain't got your friggin' money!"

James Wood brought the truck to a stop at the traffic light. They were now near downtown Alton, and there were several cars at the intersection.

"If you don't believe me," she screamed, "just drive me to the police station, and we'll go inside and let 'em shake me down!"

"I ain't driving you nowhere, bitch!" he snapped, leaning across and throwing her door open. "I'm cuttin' you loose. Just get the fuck outta my truck!"

The woman stepped into the street and slammed the truck door behind her.

"You're crazy, man! You know that? You're fuckin' crazy!" she screamed at Wood through the open window. "I'm gonna get your license number and turn your ass in for rape!" she shouted, running toward the back of the truck.

Wood was seething. He scrambled out of the cab and rushed to the rear of the truck, blocking the woman's view of his license plate. In full view of the stunned drivers behind them, Wood shoved the woman backward. The two of them stood in the middle of the street, shouting obscenities at each other. Suddenly Wood moved toward her, rage showing in his eyes. The woman backed away. Wood glared at her. Then he got back in the cab and gunned the pickup through the intersection.

Bitches like her are always causing me trouble. For the first time in my life, I had it made! I was teaching art classes, I was painting, I had a future with Yvonne, I had a new life! I was the man of the house, and my own stepdaughter wouldn't mind me! She got what she deserved, by God! She should've changed out of those clothes like I told her! But then she has to run and tell Yvonne I did it with her! She betrayed me to Yvonne, and now I've lost everything! Yvonne should just forgive and forget. If that girl had minded me in the first place, nothing would've happened! And Yvonne, damn her soul, she had to go tell the law. And then some bitch comes along and rolls me for the last bit of money I had! Now I've lost everything, dammit, every single thing I had!

A few minutes after he tossed out the biker girl, James Wood drove across the Clark Bridge, heading back into Missouri. The Sunday morning traffic was light as the Ford Ranger pickup sped across the gleaming steel and concrete structure that spanned the Mississippi River.

But James Wood was in no mood to enjoy the view from high above the mighty river on that crisp, clear fall morning. Even after finding the money in his shirt pocket—the biker gal hadn't rolled him after all—he was burning with anger, as he had been for most of his life. His anger was directed toward women. Now his mind raged over the latest disobedience of his fourteen-year old step-daughter. It was her fault that he'd lost his home and his two-and-a-half-year-old son. Up 'til now, life for Wood had been relatively good for the past five years. He had met and married Yvonne not long after his release from Louisiana's infamous Angola State Penitentiary. It had been his second stay at Angola, where he had served six years of a ten-year sentence for robbery and rape. Ironically, he was released early for good behavior.

A mutual friend had introduced Wood to Yvonne, the woman who would become his third wife. They had hit it off almost immediately. Yvonne knew the man who was soon to be her husband had been in prison at Angola, although Wood never told her that he had been there for rape. But Yvonne had been accepting, understanding, saying that everyone makes mistakes in life. Yvonne bore him a son, his third child from three marriages. Together, he and Yvonne built a modest house on several acres in the lush, green countryside outside Shreveport, Louisiana.

Damn! If only Yvonne's daughter would have obeyed him and changed out of those sexy, revealing clothes! He had made her pay for not minding, made her pay the same way he had made women pay all his adult life. He raped her. As far as he was concerned, she had gotten exactly what she deserved. Wood simply could not understand why she told Yvonne what he had done. How could she have told on him when he was only disciplining her, like any good father?

Yvonne had confronted him, asked him to leave, and said she was going to call the law. He then decided to leave his house, leave his son, leave everything. But before he left, there were things he needed. He grabbed his wife's Montgomery Ward credit card and her little Jennings .22 semiautomatic she kept in the glove compartment of her car. He threw a few other things in the back of his truck—art supplies, the set of tattoo needles he had made at Angola—and left, not even taking the time to pack clothes. Wood knew what another rape charge would mean for someone who had already been imprisoned twice. He had to get as far away from Louisiana as he could. He would go back to Idaho.

On the way out of town, he stopped at the Montgomery Ward auto center and had his truck tuned up, the oil changed, and new tires put on, getting it ready for the long drive. While he was waiting, he went inside the main store and bought socks, underwear, and several changes of clothes. He also bought a blue nylon duffel bag to put them in, charging everything to Yvonne's credit card.

Instead of heading west toward Idaho, Wood took a detour, driving north to St. Louis, several hundred miles out of his way. Wood himself was not sure why he had decided to go through St. Louis. True, his first wife Terry and his daughter and granddaughter lived in suburban St. Louis, but they were of no value to him. Wood liked to use people. He didn't care about anyone but could mimic caring if it worked to his advantage.

2

Hazelwood, Missouri. Sunday, October 25, 1992. Jeanne Faser hadn't noticed James Wood watching her from the shadows. She released the nozzle of the gas hose just as the digital readout on the pump stopped at exactly ten dollars. She replaced the gas cap and started toward the food mart to pay.

As she walked across the asphalt parking lot, her eyes met those of a man in the shadows. He was sitting in the cab of a small pickup with the door open. He was middle aged and wore a dark cap. Jeanne forced a polite smile, then averted her eyes. She opened the glass door and stepped up to the counter.

"Hi. Ten dollars for the Camaro on pump four," she said, placing a twenty-dollar bill on the counter. "May I have a ticket for the car wash, too?"

The young clerk counted back her change and handed her a receipt.

Jeanne tucked the change into her billfold and headed across the concrete apron. Just as she started to open the car door, she noticed a movement out of the corner of her eye. As she turned to look, the man who had been staring at her stepped from behind the gas pumps. In an instant he pressed against her, trapping her against the open car door.

"Get in the car," he said calmly, pulling his jacket open to reveal the butt of a pistol tucked into the waistband of his jeans.

Her eyes wide with disbelief, Jeanne looked at the silver gun, then back at the man's face. "Oh, my God!" she screamed. Before she could scream again, the man took her arms and pulled them tight behind her back.

"Shut up, or I'll kill you!" he said, the chilling tone in his voice stunning the teenager into silence. He pulled the pistol from his waistband and jammed the muzzle into her rib cage. "Get in the car!"

Jeanne slumped into the driver's seat. Oh, God, this can't be happening! This can't be happening to me, she thought.

"Move over!" the stranger ordered, sliding into the seat with her, forcing her to scramble over the console to the passenger's seat. He locked the passenger's door and cranked up the car.

Jeanne stared blankly at the key in the ignition, her house keys dangling as if in slow motion. Why did she leave the keys in the car? On North Lundberg, cars moved by on the busy four-lane highway. In a dreamlike haze, Jeanne looked back toward the food mart. Surely the cashier inside would see! Inside the brightly lit store she could see the young clerk. But he was facing away from her.

Suddenly the Camaro moved forward. The man checked for oncoming traffic, then darted onto the busy four-lane highway. Now they were alone in the car. He paced their speed so that every traffic light was green as they approached. The Camaro never stopped.

Wood looked over at the terrified young woman, her blue eyes wild with fear. "Don't worry," he said in a calm voice, looking back at the road. "I'm not going to hurt you. I just need to borrow your car for a while. I just shot somebody at a jewelry store over at a shopping center, and I've got some mechanical problems with my truck." Wood paused for a moment to let the words *I just shot somebody* sink in. He could almost see the teenager's will to resist fade from her eyes.

"Look," he said, "I'm sorry about taking your car. I'll just borrow it long enough to get away from here. When I do, you'll get it back. So you just relax and do what I say. If you do, I promise nothing's gonna happen."

As he talked, Jeanne caught the stale odor of beer on the man's breath. He's been drinking! He's been drinking, and he shot somebody! Why, God, why is this happening to me? she wondered.

"Please! Just take the car," she said, her voice breaking. "You can have the car, but please, just let me go!"

Wood eased off the accelerator and braked. As the Camaro slowed, he steered into the turn lane and crossed over into the parking lot of a car wash. A deep sense of longing knotted the pit of Jeanne's stomach as she recognized the car wash. It was owned by a friend of her stepfather. Without stopping, the man circled back onto the highway. They were going back in the direction of the food mart.

Again, Wood looked over at the terrified young girl in the passenger seat. Now, he studied her thick, dark hair and the curve of her slender neck. She had the beautiful, soft skin of a teenage girl. *Look at her. She's got class, not some trashy bitch. I'll bet she's got nice things on under them clothes, things I like. I'm gonna have her. She's got all the stuff I like.*

"You're really pretty, you know that?" he said. "Sure you do...you know you're pretty."

Jeanne didn't respond. The stranger drove on, continuing to talk as if conversing with a date. "I used to come here a lot," he said, nodding his head as they passed through a heavily developed intersection. "Things sure have changed."

"Please," Jeanne begged, desperately searching for some sign of pity in the driver's unforgiving face. "I've got to hurry home. My parents are waiting for me. They're expecting me to get gas and come right back!"

He gave her a hard look, but said nothing. Instead, he patted the butt of the gun in his belt. He reached into the pocket of his jacket and brought out what was left of his money. "See this?" he asked, holding the money out to her. "I got it from the jewelry store. You want some of it? Go ahead. Take some."

I don't take stolen money," she said defiantly.

"Suit yourself," he said, placing the money back in his pocket.

Now the gas station came back into view. For an instant, the teenager believed the man was taking her back. But the Camaro did not slow down, and Jeanne watched with resignation as the gas station slipped past. Her paralyzing despair returned. She closed her eyes and shook her head as if trying to awaken from a bad dream. This is not happening! This is not real. This cannot be happening to me, she thought to herself. But when she opened her eyes, her abductor was still there.

"Can I ask you something," she pleaded. "Why did you pick me? Why are you doing this to me?"

"I don't know," the driver answered, glancing over at her. "I guess you was just in the wrong place at the wrong time." And he drove on, following what seemed an aimless route before finally turning onto a busy divided highway leading to the nearby township of Florissant.

Jeanne tried to make mental notes of the streets and landmarks they passed. When they were going north on Interstate 170, she saw overhead expressway signs for the St. Louis International Airport. Later, on an exit ramp feeding onto McDonnell Way, they passed blue-and-white directional signs for the giant McDonnell-Douglas aircraft assembly plant. From there they drove west, following a two-lane asphalt road that took them deeper into the dismal gray countryside.

Only an occasional car whispered past in the growing twilight. Jeanne sensed the worst was yet to come. She imagined her parents were worried because she was not yet home. It was almost dark. She had promised to be home early. Oh, God, she wanted so much to be home with them. If she hadn't taken the Camaro, if she hadn't stopped for gas, if she hadn't gone to her boyfriend's apartment, none of this would be happening! She had to think of some way to stop this. More tears coursed down her cheeks. And then a thought came to her. She should pray. Pray for herself. Pray for her parents. Pray for her life. If he knew she was praying, maybe he'd feel bad about doing this. Maybe he would let her go.

"Do you mind if I pray?"

The driver looked at her. "Why?" he asked. "You religious?"

"Yes," she answered weakly, caressing the small cross that dangled from her necklace.

"What church you belong to?"

"Catholic."

"Catholic," Wood said, as though thinking out loud. He looked at the young girl, then back at the road. "Personally, I don't believe in God."

A small gravel road came into view as they neared an isolated steel bridge leading over the rain-swollen Missouri River. Wood turned sharply. Gravel crunched beneath the tires as the car left the highway. They drove slowly, following the narrow road as it took them deeper into an open field of broom sedge. At the edge of the field, a railroad trestle spanned the muddy river. The driver pulled the Camaro into a small clearing and turned off the ignition. Total silence. In the distance Jeanne could see a glowing halo of lights against the evening sky. A softball field. Not a mile away, people were playing softball under bright lights.

Wood looked at her with a wild, hungry look in his eyes. "Get in the back," he said.

Jeanne cried softly. She did not move.

The bitch doesn't want anything to do with me! She thinks she's too damn good for me! I'll show her. "I said, get in the back!"

Again the rage in his voice broke the teenager's will to resist. Scrambling, half crawling, sobbing, she slid over the console into the cramped back seat of the Camaro. She backed as far away from him as she could.

"Please, mister, just do what you want," she said through sobs. "Just don't hurt me. Please don't hurt me."

"Do what I say or I'll kill you right now!"

She became nauseous at the stench of his unwashed body. She turned her face away as he fought to kiss her.

"Kiss me, dammit! Kiss me!" he said, grabbing her hair with both hands, forcing her face to meet his. His warm breath was foul with the stale odor of cigarettes and beer.

As Jeanne sensed the inevitable, instinct told her compliance might save her life.

And then finally, it was over.

I did it, by God, I took it! She thinks she's too good for me, but by God, I showed her!

Wood picked up the pistol he had laid on the floorboard, opened the door and got out. Jeanne lay sobbing, curled in a fetal position, on the back seat.

"Get up and get your clothes on," he said, flinging her clothes at her. "I said get up and get your clothes on!"

Brushing away tears, Jeanne did as she was told.

Wood sat in the driver's seat, watching her as she dressed. "Come on up here," he said when she had finished, his voice calm again. Jeanne hesitated, then slowly crawled over the console and into the passenger seat. She huddled against the door as he started the engine, easing the Camaro back onto the small gravel road. He drove forward a few feet. Then, almost as an afterthought, Wood stopped and killed the engine.

"OK," he said calmly. "I'm goin' to let you go now, then I'm gonna park your car where the cops or somebody will find it and get it back to you. First, I need to get you far enough away from the car so I have time to go." He looked directly into Jeanne's eyes. "Got it?"

"Please, just let me go. Please take the car, take my money."

"Is that clear?"

"Yes."

"All right, now let's get out."

She unlocked her door.

"No, get out on this side. Scoot on over here." He got out and stood outside the car.

Jeanne slid across to the driver's seat. As she did, he reached down and took her arm to help her out. She felt his fingers tighten as she stood up. His grip was firm enough to control her, yet somehow it seemed strangely gentle, as if he were trying not to hurt her.

Come on with me, you fucking bitch. I'll show you!

"Come on, let's go this way," he said in his soothing voice, leading her away from the car and into the field of broom and sedge. At the edge of the field, a thick stand of trees formed a silhouette against the pale western sky. The grass was wet and slippery from the recent autumn rains. Suddenly she stumbled, her foot tangled in the branches of a dead tree limb that lay hidden in the tall grass. As she started to fall forward, he caught her and pulled her up by the arm. When she regained her balance, he gently led her forward. They walked through the field in silence. The wet grass rustled beneath their feet.

As they neared the trees, Jeanne's attacker let go of her arm. He dropped back and took the silver pistol from his belt. Then he stopped.

Jeanne walked on. She knew he had stopped.

"OK," he said from behind her.

She turned to face the voice. He was holding the pistol in front of him at eye level. He had an eerie smirk on his face.

"It's time to say good-night," he said.

"Oh, my God!" she cried, trying to turn away as

the air itself seemed to explode in a brilliant orange flash.

The young girl's legs buckled as she slumped into the tall grass. Blood trickled from a small, dark hole behind her left ear into the soft, moist earth.

3

James Wood drove west on Interstate 70, passing through the western outskirts of St. Louis. The late Sunday evening traffic was still heavy. James Wood had always liked the anonymity of traveling the interstate highways, especially those in the vast Midwest and West, where it was possible to drive for hours on end and see few signs of civilization or law enforcement. Running into lawmen in Missouri was the last thing he wanted. Less than half an hour after shooting Jeanne Faser in Bridgeton, he had driven her Camaro back to the gas station where he abducted her and robbed the place. Terrifying the young cashier at gunpoint, Wood had made off with more than $300. He now had enough cash for at least three or four days.

Tired, he began searching for an exit and a motel. Soon he would be on the open plains west of the city, where the distance between each exit grew farther with the passing miles. He searched the blackness above each approaching overpass until he saw the red-and-white Ramada Inn sign. He left the interstate and let momentum take him up the exit ramp, then turned toward the Ramada Inn. He parked on the side of the motel so that his truck could not be seen from the road.

At the desk, Wood filled out a registration card in his compulsively neat handwriting. He signed his full name, James Edward Wood. He wrote down the address of the home he had left three days earlier in Grand Cane, Louisiana. When he finished the registration card, he paid cash for the room, $49.00 plus $6.92 in tax, and asked if there were any rooms available on the ground floor. The night clerk gave him the key to room 118.

Before he went to bed on the night of October 25, 1992, Wood placed a call to his former wife Angie Bell, in nearby suburban High Ridge, Missouri.

Angie came to the phone. Twenty-five years earlier, Angie had been introduced to a young "Jim" Wood by a friend. She had become pregnant almost immediately, barely two months later they were married. Less than six months later, Angie learned her new husband had been arrested in Louisiana. He had been charged with slitting the throats of two women in their apartment and with raping one of them. The charges were later reduced to assault and battery. Still, her new husband would spend four and a half years at Louisiana's Angola State Penitentiary. Angie filed for divorce while Jim was in prison,

but they were remarried shortly after his release.
Within months she filed for a second and final divorce. Their two marriages had produced two children, a boy and a girl.

"Jim?" she asked, "Where are you?" Since their
divorce, she never knew when or from where he
would call.

"At the Ramada in St. Charles."

"How long are you here for?"

Wood hesitated. "Not sure, exactly," he answered. "The job market's not too good in Louisiana.
I'm on my way out to Idaho, thinking about looking
for work out there."

As long as she had known James Wood, he had
never been able to hold a job or stay in one place
for any length of time. Even when they were living
together, he had worked as a truck driver most of
the time, taking big rigs on interstate trips, leaving
home for weeks on end. But this was the first time
she had heard him talk about going back to Idaho,
where his mother had moved after his father went to
federal prison. Jim was two years old at the time. But
in all the years Angie had known him, Wood had
always talked about bad memories of Idaho. His
mother had remarried shortly after they moved to
Pocatello. Jim's stepfather, he often told her, had
abused him.

When he was eight years old, Wood said, he had
watched from a schoolroom window across the road
as flames consumed a potato processing plant in a
fire that killed his mother. As far as Angie knew, Jim
Wood had not been back to Idaho since getting out

of reform school when he was seventeen. One of the conditions of his release had been that he leave the state and live with his natural father in Louisiana. Later he and his father moved to St. Louis, where his father started a business selling and installing chain-link fences. Jim was working for his father when he met Angie.

"What I was hoping to do," Wood continued, "is to visit for a while tomorrow. I'd really like to see Julie if I could."

Julie was James Wood's four-year-old grand-daughter, his daughter Carolyn's only child. Although Wood had lived in dozens of towns scattered across the South and Midwest since their final divorce in 1974, he had always managed to stay in contact with his daughter and Angie. His daughter knew he had served time in prison, but she didn't know why.

"Well, the only time I know of is tomorrow afternoon," Angie said. She knew her husband didn't like Wood and didn't want him to come to their house. "Carolyn's working at a craft fair at Julie's school in the afternoon. I told her I'd meet them about four."

"Where is it?" Wood asked.

"At the elementary school on Valley Vista. You remember where it is?"

"I'll find it," Wood replied.

"Well, then, why don't we just meet by the main door about four?"

"I'll be there," he said.

At 4:00 the next afternoon, James Wood was on Interstate 70, traveling west toward Kansas City. Before leaving, he had called Angie and told her he would not be able to visit with her and their granddaughter that afternoon. He had lied, telling her that he was having mechanical troubles with the truck. He had promised to keep in touch and give their daughter a call once he got settled in Idaho. There was a little truth to what he had said about the truck. The clutch was beginning to slip because it was just plain worn out. With a little luck, he could make the 1,400 or so miles to Idaho.

In a sense, life had come full circle for James Wood. Whatever his life had become, the seeds had been sown as a child growing up in rural southeastern Idaho. Riding with him on that last, desperate journey were his personal demons, the end products of a depraved existence that included unspeakable horrors he had inflicted upon total strangers and a dysfunctional childhood he claimed was tainted with mental, physical, and sexual abuse.

4

Bridgeton, Missouri, Monday, October 26, 1992. Jerry Chadwell, along with his sixty-one-year old mother and his dog, were out for a drive on a beautiful fall afternoon. As they drove along Missouri Bottom Road, they passed a large, open field. From the road Jerry could see the old, abandoned Rock Lake fishing camp, a forlorn, weathered, wood-frame building, the doors and windows long since boarded up. It was an isolated area, where people often dumped trash.

"I'll stop here to let the dog out," Jerry said to his mother.

Jerry pulled over on the shoulder. The dog jumped out, bounding into the tall weeds. As the dog ran ahead of them, Jerry and his mother walked leisurely behind.

Suddenly, the dog stopped, its haunches up, its

front legs outstretched, barking excitedly at something in the weeds directly ahead. They could see
something a few feet directly in front of the dog but
could not make out what it was.

"Looks like another dog," his mother said.

"I don't think that's a dog," Jerry said. "You stay
back here a minute I'm gonna go see what it is."

As he made his way through the tall grass, Jerry
called to his dog. "Come here, fella. It's all right.
Come here!"

Then Jerry came to a dead stop. About fifteen
feet away a young woman was sitting on the ground,
gazing straight ahead, oblivious to both him and the
dog. Jerry could see streaks of what appeared to be
dried blood on the girl's face. He thought the young
woman looked about twenty years old. As he drew
nearer, he could see that her long brown hair was
matted with mud and dried blood. To Jerry it appeared the woman had been severely beaten.

"Are you all right?" he asked cautiously.

The young woman sat motionless in the grass,
her arms resting on her legs. She seemed to be in
shock.

"What's your name?" Jerry asked. "What are you
doing out here? Can you tell me what happened?"

No response. He saw that she was wearing only
one shoe, an open-toed black sandal. Her legs, face,
and arms were covered with dried mud. Her skin
was covered with dozens of red welts from insect
bites.

"Come here, Mama," he called. "It's a girl, and it
looks like somebody beat her up real bad."

"Oh, my goodness!" his mother said, as she hurried through the grass.

"Stay here with her," Jerry said. "I'm gonna go call somebody."

Pulling his reluctant dog by the collar, Jerry ran back to the car. He rushed to the nearest place that had a phone, the offices of the Norvel Construction Company on Missouri Bottom Road. There he called the police. A few minutes later, as Jerry waited outside in the parking lot, an officer of the Bridgeton Police Department arrived.

"There's a girl just sitting out in a field over there," Jerry said, pointing in the direction of the field. "I left my mother with her. Just follow me, and I'll show you where she is."

With the officer following, Jerry drove back to where he had found the injured woman. The officer ran ahead to the young woman. He looked into her eyes. She stared blankly ahead. One pupil was dilated more than the other, indicating that she had suffered a head injury. The officer asked the young woman her name but got no response. He sprinted back to his patrol car and radioed for assistance and a life support vehicle from the Robertson Fire District. Within minutes, several other law enforcement units and an ambulance arrived.

As paramedics rushed to attend to the injured young woman, officers checked the REGIS missing persons file. The injured girl's approximate age, hair color, clothing, and a ring on her left thumb matched those of a teenager listed as missing in a report filed only hours earlier by the St. Ann Police Department.

The young woman was identified as Jeanne Faser, age seventeen.

Meanwhile, the paramedics immobilized the injured girl's head with a cervical collar. After attaching EKG electrodes to monitor her heart, an IV was begun. Still motionless, she was strapped to a backboard and placed on a stretcher. Then the ambulance sped toward the emergency room at DePaul Community Health Center.

As Jeanne lay on the gurney in the brightly lit emergency room, she slipped in and out of consciousness. Meanwhile, her parents arrived at the hospital after what had certainly been the longest and most agonizing night of their lives.

After emergency room medical personnel had determined the young woman was bleeding near her left ear, X-rays of her head were ordered. As Jeanne was cleaned and prepped for X-rays, the attendants noticed that for the first time since she'd was found in the field, the young woman appeared to be responding to the voice of an emergency room technician. The technician leaned close to Jeanne, telling her that her parents were there, reassuring her that she would be fine. Jeanne's eyes seemed to brighten and focus. The technician was able to establish a rudimentary form of communication, directing Jeanne to squeeze her hand or blink her eyes in response to questions.

As Jeanne awaited surgery, a detective of the Bridgeton Police Department took the girl's parents aside. It was important, he said, that he attempt to question their daughter. Perhaps by blinking or squeezing their hands, Jeanne could at least give them enough information to begin a search for the person who shot her.

"Jeanne," the technician said, holding the young woman's hand as she lay on the hospital gurney, tubes in her nose, an IV in her arm. "Jeanne, if you understand me, I want you to squeeze my hand once for yes and two times for no. Can you do that for me?"

Jeanne's eyes seemed to focus. She squeezed the technician's hand once.

"Did someone rape you?

One squeeze. "Yes."

"Were you raped last night?"

Two Squeezes. "No."

"Were you hurt at the apartment on Douglas Court?" The technician had learned from her parents that Jeanne's boyfriend lived there.

Two squeezes. "No."

The questions were interrupted. It was time for Jeanne's X-rays. They revealed the teenager had been shot just behind the left ear. Perhaps because Jeanne had instinctively turned away at the instant the shot was fired, the small-caliber bullet had fragmented, the major portion traveling along her left jawline, finally lodging below the bone of her left jaw. Smaller bullet fragments had lodged in her brain.

While Jeanne was being prepared for surgery, the technician, again at the detective's directions, asked the teenager more questions.

"Jeanne, do you know who hurt you?"

Again the young woman squeezed her hand once. "Yes."

"Was more than one person involved?"

"Yes."

"Were there two people?"

"Yes."

"Do you know the second person?"

Jeanne squeezed her hand twice. "No."

Finally, the technician asked, "Jeanne, did your boyfriend shoot you?

Jeanne squeezed once. "Yes."

"Oh my God" the technician exclaimed looking up at the detective. "She squeezed my hand so hard it hurt!"

5

After a quick breakfast at a McDonald's the next morning, James Wood got on the road early, traveling across Kansas and onto the rolling prairies of eastern Colorado. Later that afternoon he reached the outskirts of Denver and turned north on Interstate 25. With the pale silhouette of the Rocky Mountains in view, Wood decided to stop for the night. Again choosing a well-developed exit with a choice of motels, restaurants, and convenience stores, he turned in at the Hacienda Motel. It was a good location, he decided. There was a Pizza Hut and several other fast-food restaurants just down the street. Wood paid cash for one night, then took his duffel bag to his room. Later, he walked back to the lobby of the motel and went into the lounge.

It was dark inside. When his eyes adjusted to the low light Wood went to the bar and sat down. To avoid attracting attention as a lone stranger, he began to mingle with the most convenient, friendly face there. Within a few minutes, he had struck up a conversation with an off-duty desk clerk from the motel. She was having a drink at the bar, waiting for friends to join her.

"What brings you to the Hacienda Motel?" the clerk asked, after the two had introduced themselves.

"Well," Wood said, "I'd been living down in Louisiana for a few years, but then Hurricane Andrew came through and wiped me out." In typical Wood fashion, he lied to gain the woman's sympathy. As always, his lies were unverifiable. "Now I'm on my way west, gonna try and find a job, start over."

"Oh, no, not another one," his new friend said, shaking her head in disbelief. "I don't know how many folks we've had come through here that got wiped out by Andrew!"

Later the clerk's friends arrived, threading their way through the crowded tables to the bar. The desk clerk introduced Wood to her friends and invited him to join them at a table. Wood gladly accepted. There was a good crowd in the lounge. The dark, smoke-filled room was full of loud conversation and country music from a jukebox. Before long, Wood began buying rounds for everyone at the table. But after a couple of rounds, he was almost out of money. He had spent almost all the $300 he had taken in the gas station robbery in Missouri. Wood knew he had to have more money soon, and he knew how he would get it.

"Darlin'," he asked the desk clerk, "you think you might be able to get me a weekly rate at the motel?"

"Why, you planning on staying around for a while?" the clerk asked.

"Maybe," Wood lied. "I like Colorado." He had no intention of remaining in Colorado, but he wanted the off-duty desk clerk to believe so. If she thought he was going to stay, she would be less likely to connect him with what he was about to do.

"Honey, I can't guarantee anything," the clerk smiled, "But I'll work on getting you a better rate when I go on duty in the morning."

Wood looked at his watch and excused himself from the table. "I'll be right back," he said politely to the group at the table.

Wood walked outside to his truck. At the far end of the motel property was the Pizza Hut, the red-and-black logo shining brightly in the night sky. On the other side of the Pizza Hut, rows of used cars lined a car lot. The lot had already closed for the night. Wood parked his truck behind a row of cars, took a canvas bank bag from behind his seat, and walked to the restaurant.

A teenaged boy was alone at the cash register. Wood placed the bank bag next to the cash register, reached into his pocket, and drew out the silver Jennings semiautomatic. "Open the register and put the folding money in the bag," he said calmly.

The color draining from his face, the young cashier did exactly as he was told. He opened the cash drawer and stuffed the money into the unzipped canvas bag. Wood took the bank bag and walked out of the door. No stress, no anxiety or guilt for Wood. In his mind, he simply had done what he needed to do. He drove back to the Hacienda Motel.

In less than ten minutes, Wood returned with nearly $700. He rejoined the clerk and her friends.

"I had to go up to my room for a minute," Wood said, ordering another round of drinks.

A few minutes later, the conversation was interrupted by the piercing sound of sirens. Patrol cars wheeled into the parking lot of the nearby Pizza Hut. The desk clerk glanced at Wood, as if debating the possibility that the soft-spoken stranger might be connected with what was going on outside. But Wood showed no nervousness or distraction. She shrugged and took another sip of her drink. The animated conversation around the table continued. Wood finished the drink he was nursing, said goodnight, and went to his room.

Early the next morning, Wood was on the road again, this time under gray, threatening skies as he drove north on Interstate 25 toward Cheyenne, Wyoming. Two hours later he turned west onto Interstate 80. Soon the Ford Ranger was climbing steadily as he made his way over high mountain passes in the Medicine Bow National Forest. At the higher elevations, what had been a steady drizzle turned to sleet. The heavy gray clouds seemed to swallow the interstate.

Already slowed by the icy conditions and poor visibility, the traffic on Interstate 80 came to a crawl east of Laramie, then stopped altogether. Somewhere ahead on the sleet-and-ice-covered freeway, two big rigs had crashed. The state police had closed the interstate until the wreckage was cleared.

More than two hours later, inching along in the freezing gray sleet, James Wood surveyed the aftermath of the truck crash as he slowly drove past the wreckage. *Somebody must have died in that one.* The traffic began to thin out and pick up speed.

Off and on throughout his adult life, Wood had worked as a truck driver. His last trucking job, shortly after his release from prison in Louisiana, was driving a tractor-trailer rig for a carnival out of Tyler, Texas. Wood had wanted to be a trucker since childhood, a dream he shared with his counselor at St. Anthony's Youth Correction Center in Idaho when he was fourteen. Although his father had wanted him to become a lawyer, Wood's ambition had always been to drive a truck like Uncle Gene. He was referring to Gene Wood, who together with his wife Mildred adopted the young James Godwin after his mother died in the fire. Young James took their name shortly after his adoption.

James Wood had planned to make it from Colorado to Idaho in about twelve hours, but weather and the truck crash delayed his arrival by several hours. It was dark by the time he passed Wyoming's famous Little America, a huge, brightly lit complex featuring restaurants, western souvenir shops, convenience stores and a motel billed as North America's largest travel center. A few miles west of Little America, Wood's pickup sped under a sign reading: U.S. 90 to Pocatello.

There, in the inky blackness of this remote region, Wood left the interstate and followed the desolate, two-lane highway, cutting across southwestern Wyoming and into Idaho. Passing through a few small towns along the highway, Wood drove on in the darkness, the highway following the Bear River as it wound through a fertile valley. Near Soda Springs, Idaho, the highway began to climb steeply as it crossed the northern end of the Wasatch Range. The highway descended just as a sharply on the western slope, leveling off and passing through the small mountain tourist town of Lava Hot Springs. Now Wood was only some twenty miles south of Pocatello.

After an absence of more than twenty-five years from rural southeastern Idaho, James Edward Wood was returning home. Unfortunately for Wood, "home" didn't stir longings or wishful desires to revisit his past. It was simply a familiar place where he had relatives he could use.

6

---

ocatello, Idaho. Fall 1992. Driving north on Interstate 15 from Salt Lake City at night, Pocatello appears suddenly from the high-desert
blackness. Below, argon streetlights sweep across
the floor of the Portneuf Valley. The lights follow the
incline of the land, rising gently in the west, where
sprawling subdivisions climb the foothills on the
eastern slope of the Pocatello Range. Somber mountains carpeted with prairie grass and gray-green sagebrush rise both to the east and west. The valley floor
is rich with trees on an otherwise treeless landscape.
Pocatello itself lies at the northern end of the valley.
The cityscape is dominated by Idaho State University's Holt arena. On the western edge of town, huge
grain elevators tower above the rail yards.

Pocatello owes its existence to transportation,
first as a corridor for stage lines and later as a major

rail junction for the Union Pacific Railroad, still one of the city's largest employers. Other major employers of Pocatellans are the nearby government nuclear research center and two local hospitals. The city center's two main streets are lined with shops and eateries housed in turn-of-the-century brick buildings that could easily serve as a backdrop for a 1920s movie set. Today, access to the interstates drives Pocatello's commercial growth. At the north end of town, where Yellowstone Avenue crosses Interstate 86, is the city's newest shopping mall, anchored by J. C. Penney, The Bon Marche, and ZCMI, a Mormon-owned department store. Across the street Wal-Mart, McDonald's, Denny's, and the Flying J gas station and convenience store are universal symbols of middle-class America.

One of the most popular restaurants in Pocatello is an Italian eatery named Buddy's, a flat-roofed, cinder-block building with a lighted sign that reads Spaghetti, Ravioli, Beer. Inside, it is not unusual to see a weathered rancher in western jeans and cowboy boots having dinner with his family and, at the next table, a pair of young university students with punk hairstyles and nose rings. Regulars drop into the bar inside Buddy's on weekdays after work.

But if Pocatello is a working-class town without obvious charm, its true beauty lies in its people. Sales clerks and shop owners are friendly and attentive to the needs of their customers. Townspeople are inclined to smile at strangers. Above all, it is a city of children. Perhaps this reflects the city's large number of Mormon residents—60 percent of a population just over 50,000. Whatever the reason, children are everywhere—in malls and parks and fast-food restaurants, in their mothers' arms and at their sides, playing outside after school, and riding bicycles as they deliver the local newspaper, the *Idaho State Journal.*

James Wood sat up in the front seat as the first dim light of dawn filled the cab of his truck. He had arrived in Pocatello close to three in the morning. Tired, he had pulled onto a tree-lined residential street and parked his truck among the cars that lined the road. There he slept fitfully in the cab of his pickup. He looked around. It was his first view of Pocatello by day in over twenty-five years. Wood didn't recognize the neighborhood where he had chosen to spend the night. In fact, he would not recognize a great deal of Pocatello. But the old city center looked much as it had when he was a child.

Driving north on Yellowstone Avenue, Wood turned in at the McDonald's near the Pocatello Mall. He ordered breakfast and took his tray to a booth in the back of the dining area.

He had been seated for only a few minutes when Teton Jackie, a female disc jockey on a local country radio station, interrupted his breakfast. She was conducting a live broadcast for a breakfast promotion at McDonald's. She had already interviewed several customers when she saw one she described as a "quiet little man sitting by himself in the back."

"Good morning, sir," she said in a loud, lusty voice. She slid into the booth next to Wood, holding the wireless microphone toward him. "Are you having our breakfast special this morning?"

Looking annoyed, Wood leaned toward the microphone. "No," he said quietly. "Actually, I'd already ordered something else."

"Well," Jackie said into the microphone, getting up, "You ought to give it a try sometime!"

"I sure will," Wood said as Teton Jackie winked at him and moved on to find more a responsive customer.

Little did the morning deejay realize that the "quiet little man in the back" of McDonald's had, in fact, brutally raped and shot a teenage girl and committed two armed robberies in the past seventy-two hours.

As Wood finished his breakfast, a young policewoman and her friend sat down at a nearby booth. Wood leaned over and began to talk to them.

"Excuse me, ma'am," Wood said politely to the policewoman. "I've been away from here for about twenty-five years, and I'm trying to look up some of my relatives that live around here. I haven't seen any of them since I was gone, and I was just wondering if you might know my aunt, Amy Hill."

"Oh, my gosh, yes," smiled the officer. "I have a girlfriend who was a good friend of Amy's." Then she paused. "But Amy's dead now. She passed away several years ago."

"Well, I'll be," Wood said, sadly shaking his head. "I'm really sorry to hear that. I've been away so long I hadn't heard anything about it." After his father was sent to Leavenworth Prison when Wood was two, his mother had divorced him and later moved to Pocatello, taking young James and his half-brother with her. The three of them had lived with Amy Hill until Wood's mother remarried.

"Did you say you've got other relatives still living here?" the officer asked, taking her pen out of her uniform pocket and searching her bag for a piece of paper.

"Quite a few, cousins and all," Wood replied sadly.

"Here, let me give you my friend's telephone number," the policewoman said, writing the number on a slip of paper and giving it to Wood. "She knew Amy real well, and I'll bet she can tell you about your cousin. I think they're still living in Chubbuck, just right up the road here."

James Wood stuffed the piece of paper in his pocket. He had no intention of calling the policewoman's friend. In fact, he already knew that his aunt was dead and that several of his relatives were listed in the telephone directory. He had simply used the policewoman in an effort to appear normal. After all, would someone who had just raped and shot a young woman walk up to a police officer and begin a conversation?

Leaving McDonald's, Wood drove north on Yellowstone Avenue, eventually crossing over Interstate 86 near the new Wal-Mart and into the town of Chubbuck, Idaho, the small sister city of Pocatello. There he stopped at a coin-operated laundry in a small strip mall and washed his soiled clothes. While he waited, he thumbed through the directory at a pay phone. He found both Dave Haggard's number and the number for Dave's sister, Pearl. He decided to call his cousin Pearl first.

"Jimmy?" Pearl said, after Wood identified himself. She had not heard from Wood since he left
Idaho as a teenager. Wood told Pearl that he was in
Pocatello to look for work and hoped to stay at his
cousin Dave's house until he could find work.

"Where are you calling from?" she asked.

"I'm on Yellowstone Avenue," Wood said. He
described the nearby stores and a gas station.

"Well, you're real close to Dave's house", Pearl
said. She gave him directions.

On Halloween morning, 1992, Dave Haggard sat
at the kitchen table enjoying his morning cigarette
and coffee.

A stout, well-built man in his early fifties, Haggard showed the effects of decades in the dry, high-
desert climate of south eastern Idaho. He was
tanned, with deep lines etched into his neck and
face. His pale blue eyes were deeply-set. He wore
faded jeans and a white short-sleeved undershirt,
one sleeve rolled up to hold a package of Marlboros.
Tattoos of scantily clad pinup girls covered the inside of each thick forearm.

Haggard earned a living any way he could, usually from laying linoleum, supplementing that by
selling used cars and trucks. His house, on a tree-
lined country road, was a rambling affair, the pasture
beside it filled with an assortment of cars, vans, even
an old church bus. A stack of old lumber was piled
among the cars, along with two big truck tires. Haggard had recently added a redwood deck to the side

of his house, and now a red wishing well occupied one corner of the deck. An American flag flew from a short flagpole mounted on the side of the house.

Inside, the house was filled with country knick-knacks and antiques, many of them found at yard sales in Chubbuck and Pocatello, a Saturday morning routine for Haggard. In the dark paneled den, over-stuffed recliners and a big-screen projection TV covered one wall. A wood-burning stove stood along the opposite wall. In the basement, Haggard had added a couple of small bedrooms. Divorced, Haggard often welcomed relatives who needed a place to stay into his home. "We're a close family" Haggard said. "If I needed $10,000, all I'd have to do is walk over there to the corner to my brother-in-law's house, and he'd get out his checkbook and write me a check. Just like that!" He snapped his thick fingers. "At one time I had seven or eight people living here in the house. If a man needs a place to stay while he gets on his feet, why, he's welcome here."

A few minutes past seven, Dave Haggard heard a vehicle pull up. From where he was sitting, all he could see was the front of a dark-brown pickup. The driver was already walking up to the door. There was a knock. Haggard snuffed out his cigarette. He ambled through the den and opened the door. Standing on the other side of the screen door was James Wood. Dave Haggard studied Wood for a moment, trying to place him.

"You don't recognize me, do you?" Wood asked politely, extending his hand. "I'm your cousin Jim, remember?"

Haggard showed a flicker of recognition. "Jimmy boy," he said, reaching out to shake Wood's hand. "Why, I haven't seen you since I used to baby-sit you when you were just a little kid! Well, come on in, let's sit down and have a cup of coffee!"

Wood followed his cousin back to the kitchen.

"Take a seat," Dave said, pulling a chair out from the table. "Last I heard, you were in Louisiana. Is that where you drove in from?"

"Uh-huh," Wood said.

"You look a little tired. What'd you do, drive all night?"

"Just about," Wood said, settling into a chair. "There wasn't a lot of places to stay once I got off the interstate, so I just come straight on through to Pocatello."

Haggard filled a coffee mug from a large silver commercial coffee brewer on the counter. "There's cream and sugar if you take it," he said, going back to the table and handing Wood the coffee.

"Boy, it's been a while," Haggard said, sitting across from Wood. "So what in the world are you doing up here in Idaho? Last I heard, you were married and raising a family, living down in Louisiana."

"Well, I'm married, and I got a little baby boy," Wood, said, sipping the hot coffee. "And a step-daughter, by my wife. But I ain't had much luck finding work lately. The economy's real bad in Louisiana, so I'm planning on relocating out here. But to tell the truth, I've been wanting to get back out here for a long time."

"What's your wife and baby gonna do?"

"I come on out by myself, till I can find some work. Once I get back on my feet, I'm gonna bring Yvonne and the boy out."

"What kinda work you lookin' for?"

"Just about anything that pays," Wood said. "I was teaching art classes, selling some paintings, things like that. Maybe later on I can do some of that around here, but right now, I'll take just about anything."

"Well," said Dave, "I got a little business here, laying linoleum. Sometimes I can use help with that, if the job's big enough. You got any experience at layin' tile?"

"No, but I'm pretty good with my hands. I imagine I could pick it up pretty quick."

Then Wood came to the point of his visit. "By the way, you got any room here so I could stay for a while? I'd just be here long enough to get back on my feet and get Yvonne and the kids out."

"Why, sure," Haggard replied. "Grab your coffee and come on. I'll show you around the place."

With Wood trailing behind him, Haggard took his cousin on a tour of the house.

"I always keep plenty of fresh brewed coffee," Haggard said, "Just help yourself any time you want. There's food in the refrigerator. Help yourself to that, too."

On a cabinet door above the kitchen counter was a small needlepoint sign: Love, Like Bread, Should Be Made Fresh Everyday.

Haggard turned to his cousin. His gaze was direct. "There's just one house rule—no drinking. I keep a little beer in the refrigerator, but that's just for when company comes. Other than that, I don't allow drinking in the house."

Haggard led his cousin down a small flight of stairs to a narrow hallway. He opened a door at the end of the hall, showing Wood a small bedroom. Haggard flipped a switch. A bright fluorescent glow filled the room. The room was furnished with a small twin-size bed, a dresser, and a seat out of a pickup truck that now served as a sofa. The floor was covered with brown shag carpet.

"Think this'll get you by for a while?" Haggard asked, walking toward a small closet. "You can put your things in here, and whatever won't fit we can find a place for somewhere."

"Oh, this is fine," Wood said, glancing at the small room he would call home for the next nine months. "I didn't bring that much with me, anyway."

Wood proved to be a good house guest. He was compulsively neat, and he followed Haggard's rule about not drinking in the house, though he did "nurse" a beer or two while he labored in the woodworking shop in the garage. Although Wood never paid Haggard rent for the small bedroom, he did pitch in for groceries and sometimes even cooked.

"He likes to cook," Haggard told a friend. "Cooks beans a lot, pinto beans and white beans. And he cooks stews, too. He makes a good stew.

"He was just a nice guy. Ask any of the neighbors, they'll all say the same thing. He'd go out of his way to help, and he was good with the kids, too. He liked to talk, strike up a conversation. Didn't watch TV much, read a paper, or talk about politics or things like that. Just everyday conversation, just like me and anybody else. He had just a few belongings with him when he got here, but he dressed really neat. He usually wore jeans, but he was always neat. He always kept his cars clean. He was just a clean person."

Indeed, Wood kept his bedroom impeccably neat. The twin-size bed was always made. He carefully hung his shirts, slacks, and jackets in the closet. At the bottom of the closet, he lined up his worn cowboy boots, some black wing tips, a pair of black dress shoes, and leather work boots. His socks, T-shirts, and underwear were clean and folded in a dresser drawer. Tucked away under the folded clothing was a box of .22 long rifle cartridges. Out of a box of 50, more than half of the cartridges were missing.

Not long after James Wood arrived, Dave Haggard took him along on some jobs and attempted to teach Wood how to lay linoleum. But the work didn't seem to suit Wood. Although he was fairly competent at cutting the linoleum, he never mastered the art of applying the adhesive evenly or placing the linoleum precisely. Wood explained that his weak left hand may have been a factor. Three of his fingers were severely cut in an accident while he was operating a power saw in 1990. The fingers were surgically repaired, but he often complained of poor circulation in his hand. Injured hand or not, the truth was Wood didn't like to work. It was much easier to rob a store when he needed money. Work was too boring. After joining Haggard on two or three jobs, he lost interest in learning how to lay linoleum.

But Haggard and Wood soon realized they shared a common interest in garage sales. On weekends, they drove around the residential neighborhoods of Pocatello and Chubbuck, stopping at each garage sale they came across, rummaging through tables filled with odds and ends. Wood was especially interested in old handsaws and the old-fashioned metal milk cans used by dairy farmers.

When Wood found handsaws or metal jugs, he took them home and cleaned them. He removed the rust with sandpaper and wiped them down with mineral spirits. Then he set up his small, portable easel on Haggard's kitchen table. There, in the natural light from a window, he painted farm and wildlife scenes. Working in oils and using only his imagination, he used quick, precise brush strokes to develop a scene, adapting each painting to fit the shape of the object. On the old handsaws, his paintings usually featured a weathered barn in the background and a mailbox standing next to a wooden fence. He often included deer or other wildlife in the scenes. He also liked to do winter scenes. His springtime scenes were equally impressive, with lush green trees and blue skies. And always he signed his name in a compulsively neat, stylized calligraphy.

"He was the best artist I ever saw," Haggard said.

"He could paint anything. I've never seen anybody who could paint like he could. He didn't have to try to sell his stuff. People would come to him. They'd see something he did for me, and they'd want one like it. Didn't matter what they wanted, ol' Jim could paint it.

"And he could tattoo. He could tattoo just about anything you could want. Just show him what you wanted, and he'd start doing it, no sketch or anything. And it'd be perfect. He'd even made his own set of tattoo needles while he was down there in prison. He didn't work out of anybody's shop. He'd just load up his needles and things and go tattoo 'em."

7

Snow came early to Pocatello in the fall of 1992, and blizzards continued through the winter. Fierce storms blew in from the west every two weeks, or so it seemed. That year, the peaks of the tallest mountains were snow-capped until mid-summer. In late November, as the town settled into the familiar routine of winter, James Wood had adapted well to his new surroundings.

After taking a job as a dishwasher at Tina's Ox Bow restaurant, Wood used his spare time to complete a number of paintings, most of them on a collection of old handsaws he had found at the yard sales. He loaded the paintings into his truck and drove to antique shops and other businesses around Pocatello to sell them.

One of his first stops was the Pilot House Restaurant. A local landmark, the Pilot House had a reputation for its hearty portions of Mexican-American food. The restaurant was housed in a low-lying building made of weathered pine logs on open land near the huge Simplot potassium processing plant. Inside were crisp red-and-white checkered tablecloths. The waitresses wore black skirts with burgundy knit shirts. In the small bar off the dining room, Christmas lights twinkled above the rough-hewn beams of the ceiling. The log walls were covered with paintings on velvet, model airplanes, antique toys, and other memorabilia.

The owner of the Pilot House, Annie Gallegos, was a slim, immaculately dressed woman in her late sixties. Dark gray hair framed her face. She wore bright red nail polish, and a large diamond sparkled on her ring finger. An energetic woman, Annie was unmistakably the master of her ship, issuing sharp orders to her help that customers be served promptly. Still, she always found time to talk with her favorite customers.

The manager and hostess of the Pilot House was Annie's daughter Mitzi. Known by the regulars as "Little Annie," Mitzi inherited both her mother's good looks and her temperament. Annie and her daughter were as much a part of the atmosphere of the Pilot House as the Christmas lights that decorated the bar.

Wood sensed the friendly restaurant would be a good place to sell his artwork the moment he walked in. And he was right. Early one evening in mid-November, before the start of the dinner rush, he sat down at the bar and ordered a cup of coffee. Annie was behind the bar. Soon she and Wood engaged in conversation, Annie occasionally pausing to replenish Wood's cup with fresh coffee. When Annie asked Wood about his line of work, he replied that he was an artist. Annie asked Wood if he would bring some of his work by sometime. Wood said he had several paintings in his truck. He excused himself and went outside. He returned a few minutes later with two of his painted handsaws and placed them on the bar for Annie to examine.

"These are very good," she said, holding one of the saws at arm's length to admire it. It was one of Wood's farm scenes with deer in the foreground. Annie was impressed with the quality of Wood's technique and composition and called her daughter over to see the paintings. Like her mother, Mitzi marveled at the color and detail of the rustic scenes. Soon several employees gathered around, remarking on the stranger's obvious talent. Annie asked Wood how much he wanted for the painted handsaws. She bought them both. Annie placed the handsaws on a shelf behind the bar next to colorful toy cars and airplanes.

"Would you be willing to display some of my artwork in the restaurant?" Wood asked. Maybe customers would be interested."

"I'll be glad to," said Annie. "Just mark the price you want on the back, an we'll hold the money for you."

Soon, Wood became something of a fixture at the Pilot House. Dropping in every day or so to check on the sales and to bring fresh paintings. Wood sat at the bar leisurely enjoying a cup of coffee. He always engaged in polite conversation with Annie or Mitzi or whoever happened to be at the bar.

At about the same time, Wood also became a regular at the Pizza Hut on Yellowstone Avenue in Pocatello. The Pizza Hut offered economical daily luncheon specials. Wood's favorite was an individual pizza served with a small pitcher of beer. He always came in for lunch alone.

The early snowfall added to the excitement of the Christmas shopping season in Pocatello. This Saturday, the Portneuf Valley was covered with snow. The surrounding mountains were beautiful under a brilliant blue winter sky. At the Pine Ridge Mall, the Christmas decorations were up. Parking lots were full. Inside, throngs of shoppers relished the warm, festive atmosphere.

Among the thousands of shoppers at the mall was Beth Edwards, a pretty, brown-haired teenager. Beth and her mother, together with Beth's two younger brothers and her baby sister, had arrived at the mall early. After several hours of shopping, the family loaded their shopping bags into the trunk of their car. Beth pleaded with her mother to let her drive. She had just recently obtained her learner's permit. She giggled with delight when her mother agreed. Where should they have lunch? The children's vote was unanimous-the Pizza Hut on Yellowstone Avenue.

Beth steered the aging Mercury into the driveway of the Pizza Hut. She stopped by the entrance to let everyone out so they would not have to tread through the snow. Then she drove to the parking lot behind the restaurant and parked.

Inside the Pizza Hut, the Edwards family lunched

on pizza and soft drinks. Beth, finishing her lunch first, offered to warm up the car and pull around to the entrance. "OK. Please take your baby sister to the car with you," Beth's mother said. "I'll pay the tab at the register, then we'll wait at the door while you pull the car around."

 "I'll be at the door in a couple of minutes," Beth said. She wrapped her two-year-old sister in a blanket and lifted her to her shoulder. Beth then headed for the car.

Beth's mother and two brothers stood at the entrance. A few minutes had passed. Still there was no sign of Beth. Growing impatient, Beth's mother told her oldest son to go to the parking lot to see what was taking his sister so long to move the car. The young boy dashed out into the cold, then returned momentarily with a puzzled look on his face. "The car's gone," he said.

8

Scott Shaw's love of the outdoors was part of what drew him to Pocatello, Idaho. He and his young wife were living in Salt Lake City, Utah, when Shaw accepted a job with the Pocatello Police Department in 1977. His wife was a native of Idaho, and they both liked the quality of life there. Besides Pocatello was only an hour away from the Bear River, which offers great fishing as well as hunting.

At thirty-nine, Shaw was a tall, trim man with a resonate voice that commanded attention. He had received a promotion to detective four years after joining the force. Shaw soon developed a reputation as one of the department's top homicide investigators. He was often assigned to particularly difficult cases. Shaw had an uncanny ability to coax incriminating information and even confessions out of suspects.

"Shaw's an interesting study in a law enforcement officer," said Prosecutor Mark Hiedeman of Bannock County, Idaho. "He has the sort of mentality that allows him to relate to criminals, and he understands what they're saying, what they're thinking. And I think criminals, especially sociopaths, feel some sort of camaraderie with Shaw. I don't understand it, but it's true. He could get confessions and statements on cases that no other cop could. He was really good at that."

Shaw was earnest in his efforts to grow as a law enforcement officer. He had developed an intense interest in criminal profiling, especially in cases involving sexual offenders. He read every scientific journal and study he could find. He attended seminars and classes presented by professional groups and law enforcement agencies, including courses offered by the FBI's Behavioral Science Center.

As a result, he was frequently assigned cases involving adolescent and post-pubescent sexual crimes. In 1986, following allegations the department had mishandled a reported gang rape near the Idaho State University campus, Shaw developed and implemented a post puberty sexual offense protocol. The protocol was used by all officers when interviewing victims of rape or other sexual violence. By the fall of 1987, Shaw had been promoted to detective sergeant. Although he had supervisory responsibilities, he still answered to the top brass.

Shaw also had a reputation as a loner. Some of his fellow officers, while acknowledging his talent, found Shaw to be cool and aloof. Shaw saw himself as simply a quiet person, someone more comfortable alone than in crowds. His passion for hunting and fishing testified to his desire for solitude.

Still, when it came to confrontations with his supervisors, Shaw was anything but quiet. His passions and opinions about his work frequently led to verbal confrontations with his superiors. Shaw was threatened with insubordination on several occasions, usually for displaying a "disrespectful" attitude toward his superiors.

On Tuesday, December 2, 1992, Scott Shaw sat at his desk, going over offense reports that had been written over the weekend. After a rare three days off, his first task was to review the reports that had been written over the weekend. Most of the reports involved burglaries, car thefts, or drunken brawls that had gotten out of hand. But one report was different.

The report had been taken on Saturday. It listed the victim as Edwards, Beth Ann, age fifteen. Shaw leaned back in his chair and read the report filed by a colleague.

On 11/28/92, at 1603 hours (4:03 P.M.), I was dispatched to the above location on a report of an abduction where a handgun was used. Upon my arrival, I contacted Elaine Edwards who advised me that her daughter, Beth Ann Edwards, had been abducted from the parking lot at the Pizza Hut restaurant on Yellowstone. At this time I requested that the victim, Beth, be brought to the Pocatello Police Department for an interview.

The officer then summarized Beth's statement to the police. After leaving her mother and siblings inside the restaurant, Beth said she took her baby sister with her while she went outside to warm up the car. Beth was distracted for a moment as she leaned across the front seat with the door open, buckling the seat belt around her baby sister. When she rose up, Beth said, a man came to the open car door and put a small, shiny gun to her stomach. The man ordered Beth to "scoot over" and give him the car keys. He started the car and drove out of the Pizza Hut parking lot, turning right on Yellowstone Avenue. As he drove, the man told Beth he had "robbed a jewelry store" and needed her car because there had been people around his own car and he could not get to it.

The report described the man as an adult white male approximately 38 years old, 5′9″ to 5′10″ tall, 160 pounds, with short brown hair. He wore a goatee and a mustache, which Beth said came down to the corners of his mouth. The attacker was missing two upper teeth near the front. He wore jeans and a blue-jean jacket with a white fleece collar and lining. He was not wearing glasses.

After driving around for what seemed a long time, Beth said, the man drove into the foothills on the west side of town and turned off the highway into a "little circle area." Then he raped her. The report graphically described Beth's account of the attack:

> The suspect put his hands up under her bra and touched her breasts. He also sucked on

them. She stated that he also wanted her to perform oral sex on him and to kiss his private part (referring to his penis). She told me that the suspect took off her pants and panties and took his pants off and raped her.

She told him when he was raping her that he was hurting her, and he told her to "shut up." She advised me that she was bleeding due to the intercourse. He asked her, when he found she was bleeding, if she "was on the rag."

She stated that after he raped her, he got out of the vehicle and walked her up by some bushes. He told her to wait there a few minutes, that he was going to drive the car down the road, and pointed out a blue house, stating he would leave the car there.

She stated that he was nervous, telling her, "I don't trust you." He pointed the gun at her head and said, "No, I don't want to do that," and then took her back to the car. They left the area and drove around and then he took her to an area near the Syringa School, where he let her out, along with her sister Victoria. She stated that as he drove, the suspect kept saying, "I don't think you should tell anyone, I don't think it would be a good thing to do, do you?" Then, the man took Beth's gloves. He put them on and wiped the interior of the car to remove his fingerprints. When he left her near the school, he told her he would leave her car at the Pizza Hut. She walked to the

Pizza Hut and called her mother. When they returned home, they contacted the police department. She also mentioned the man was weaving all over the road and was possibly intoxicated.

The rest of the report summarized the evidence gathered by Detective Robinson, which at that point consisted only of the clothing Beth was wearing. The report noted that although Beth had changed clothing at home after locating her car near the Pizza Hut, she had not taken a bath.

Shaw paused. By design or accident, that was a lucky break. Some physical evidence such as fibers, semen, or pubic hairs from the rapist probably would have been lost if Beth had showered or bathed before an examination. Many victims who survive a rape have an overwhelming urge to shower at the first opportunity.

Reading on, Shaw learned that after collecting the clothing, Detective Robinson drove Beth and her mother to the Bannock Regional Medical Center, where a sexual assault kit was administered. The procedure included taking vaginal and rectal swabs and collecting pubic hairs. Beth was treated for vaginal trauma in the center's emergency room. After Beth was released from the medical center, Detective Robinson drove her and her mother to the foothills on the west side of Pocatello. Following the young victim's directions, they were able to locate the isolated area where the rape had occurred.

As Shaw studied the report, it seemed clear that the man who had raped Beth did not know the streets in Pocatello very well. He had turned down two dead-end streets before eventually finding a road leading into the foothills. Beth said the man became "angry" each time he realized he had turned onto a dead-end street.

Shaw was familiar with the area where the rape had occurred. As West Fremont Street climbs higher into the grass-covered foothills, the distance between the homes along the road increases. The report said the man had turned into a "circle area" off Fremont Street, near an unmanned pumping station operated by the Pocatello Water Department. Two dirt driveways lead from Fremont Street to the pump house, a drab-green brick building about the size of a small house. The two dirt driveways met at a small parking area in front of the pump house, forming the "circle area" Beth had described. Between the northern entrance to the pump house and Fremont Street was a mound of earth covered with tall, brown prairie grass. A car parked close to the mound would have been hidden from cars passing on Fremont Street.

Still, the attacker had taken a risk: he had raped the teenager in broad daylight in the front seat of her car. It was not unusual for cars or delivery trucks to use the circle to turn around. Two or three houses were visible, although none afforded a direct line of sight to where the car had been parked.

After posting an officer to secure the area, detective Robinson drove Beth and her mother home, then returned to the pump house. Parking his car along Fremont, the detective got out and walked toward the snow-covered mound of earth. He could see fresh tire tracks in the snow where Beth said the car had been parked. The man had apparently left the engine running during the rape. The exhaust had melted a small circle in the snow, turning it black. Clearly visible in the deep snow were two sets of footprints leading away from where the car had been parked to a snowbank some twenty yards away. The footprints, one set larger than the other, showed that the man had walked behind and slightly to the right of Beth. He had stopped about three feet behind her when he ordered her to kneel in the snow. Robinson saw the impressions Beth's knees had made in the snow. Both sets of footprints led back to where the car had been parked.

Shaw opened a follow-up report that was attached to Detective Robinson's original report. It was a copy of a computerized sketch based on Beth's description of the man who attacked her. The final sketch, the report noted, was said by Beth Edwards to "closely match the appearance of the man."

Shaw closed the report and put it on his desk. Aside from the horrific act it described, something else troubled him about the report. Shaw grabbed the file and walked down the hall toward Detective Robinson's office. Robinson, who commuted to work from the small, rural mountain community of Inkom, was seated behind his desk. He glanced up over his glasses at Shaw.

"Cliff," Shaw said, sitting down across from Robinson. "What do you make of this Edwards case?"

"Well, Scott," Robinson replied, leaning back in his chair. "I'm not exactly sure what to make of it."

"You think it's a false report?"

"No, I'm not saying it's a false report," Robinson insisted.

"Well, what is it, then, Cliff?" Shaw prodded. "I know something's bothering you."

Robinson paused for a moment. "Look, I know something happened, they treated her for vaginal trauma. I saw the tracks in the snow where she said it happened. But when I took the report, Scott, she showed absolutely no emotion whatsoever. Nothing. She just sat there and answered everything I asked her as calmly as you please. Everything she said was just very matter-of-fact. Didn't seem mad, didn't seem upset, nothing."

Robinson often worked on sexual and physical abuse cases for Child Protection. He had interviewed more rape and abuse victims, young and old, than he cared to remember. But never one who did not show at least some sign of emotion or anger.

"So that's what put you off, Cliff?" Shaw asked. "Because she didn't get all upset and emotional?"

"No, not exactly," Robinson said earnestly. "I guess I just don't get it. I can't imagine a kid her age going through something like that without it just making her crazy."

"What about her car?" Shaw said. "Were you able to lift any prints, anything?"

"Nothing," Robinson said. "The victim said he used her gloves to wipe everything down. She even remembered him bumping his head against the rear-view mirror while he was raping her. He had to readjust it while he was driving her back down, but he must have remembered to wipe that, too."

Shaw went back to his office and reread the report. He was convinced the department had a troubling and dangerous case on their hands, especially after learning that the man had said on at least two occasions during Beth's abduction and rape: *I'm in control.*

Shaw glanced at his watch. It was almost 8:00 P.M. He turned back to the first page of Robinson's report, found Beth's number, and called her home. Beth's mother answered. Shaw identified himself and asked to speak with Beth. He told her that he needed additional information about Beth's attack and asked if she felt like coming down to the station. "Yeah," Beth said. "I'll ask Mom to drive me down."

Waiting in his office for Beth and her mother, Shaw thumbed through the report again. *I'm in control,* the man had said. Sexual psychopaths do not rape out of a desire for sexual pleasure. They rape out of a desire to control someone by humiliating and degrading the person. Were they dealing with a sexual psychopath? He would want to ask the teenager if she had tried to escape or to attract the attention of motorists at busy intersections along Yellowstone. From the time the man abducted her until he let Beth and her sister out near the school, the teenager had been in the car with the man for well over an hour.

Shaw glanced up as a young woman in her early thirties and a teenage girl came in through the double doors. As he walked out to greet Beth and her mother, he was struck by how much alike they looked. Both had the same fine brown hair, the same round faces, the same build. More like sisters than mother and daughter, he thought. But he was also struck by how innocent and natural Beth appeared. She wore little or no makeup and was dressed casually in comfortable jeans. The young woman did not fit the mold of a typical high-risk rape victim in either appearance or dress. The thought also crossed his mind that Beth was not much older than his own daughter.

"Hello," he said, extending his hand to Beth's mother, then to Beth. "I'm Sergeant Scott Shaw." After the introductions, Shaw asked Beth's mother if she would mind waiting outside while he talked to her daughter alone.

"That's fine," she said, taking a seat near the entrance.

Shaw led Beth back to his office and closed the door. "Have a seat, Beth," he said, pulling out one of the metal chairs facing his desk. "Can I get you anything, a Coke or something?"

"No, I'm OK," Beth said quietly.

Shaw took a seat behind his desk. The room was wired for sound, and he already had a tape recorder running. "Are you getting everything you need?" he asked, putting a fresh cassette in the recorder. "Have they referred you to a counselor?"

"Yeah, it's fine," Beth said, sitting absolutely erect in the chair, her hands folded in her lap.

Shaw tested the recorder, then looked back at the

young girl. She appeared neither upset nor apprehensive.

"I can't possibly know how you feel," Shaw said, "but I've investigated enough of these crimes to have at least some understanding of what you've been through. We're going to have a frank discussion about what happened to you, and It's very important you give me honest, open answers. You can interrupt me anytime you feel the need. But remember, it's important that you give me complete, open answers, because that's the only way we're going to apprehend whoever did this to you and make sure he doesn't do it to anyone else."

Beth nodded her head.

"I hope you won't feel embarrassed," Shaw continued, "Just remember, you're not going to say anything I haven't heard before or anything that's going to embarrass me. Is that OK with you?"

"Yeah," Beth said shyly.

Shaw began with questions about how the man had initially taken control of the young girl. Beth described how the man had walked up to the open car door as she was putting her baby sister in the seat belt and had placed the barrel of the pistol to her stomach. She had not seen from what direction he had come, but thought it was from somewhere in the Pizza Hut parking lot.

"OK. What did he say when he pointed the pistol at you?"

"Scoot over."

"And you did what he said?"

"Uh huh. I slid over and put my sister in my lap."

"Then what?"

"He told me to put the keys in."

"In the ignition?"

"Yeah, but I didn't do it, so he just snatched them out of my hand and started the car."

She had passively resisted by not putting the keys in the ignition. Still, she had not screamed or attempted to attract attention.

"Did he use physical force to control you, to make you do what he said?" he asked.

"He made me move over with the gun." Beth said.

"How did he keep control over you after that?"

"He told me he didn't want to hurt me. He said he'd robbed a jewelry store and he just needed my car to go somewhere to meet his partner. And I knew he had the gun," Beth stated matter-of-factly. "I was just scared. I was scared the whole time."

"What did he do with the gun after he was in the car?"

"He put it in his back pants pocket."

Shaw wanted to know how the man had maintained control over Beth while he was driving. "Did you ever think about resisting, maybe trying to get out of the car when he stopped at a traffic light?"

"Not with my little sister in the car," Beth said. "And he told me he wasn't going to hurt me."

"Did he ask you for your name?"

"He asked me my name and where I lived. I made up a name and told him I lived on Buckskin Road," Beth replied.

"OK, during the actual attack when he raped you

I want you to describe the physical force he used. At what point in the attack did he use it?"

"The first time, I guess, was when he pointed the gun at me. I was afraid."

"What about at the time he actually assaulted you, after you were parked?"

"My sister was asleep by then, and he told me to put her the back seat," she explained. "Then he told me to slide over and sit next to him, but I didn't. I just stayed on my side of the car. So he reached over and grabbed me by my hair and pulled me over. He made me sit in his lap."

"So he used your hair to force you over?" Shaw asked. "Exactly where did he grab you by your hair?"

"Just right behind my neck."

"OK, after he pulled you over by your hair, did he release it or keep holding it?"

"No, once I was over in his lap, he let go of my hair."

The man had used just enough force to control the frightened young girl, to make her slide over beside him. But he hadn't used enough to really hurt her.

"And what did he do at that point?"

"He put his hands under my bra," Beth said. "But I tried to push his hands away."

"You tried to remove his hand from your breast?"

"Yeah."

"What was his reaction?"

"He told me not to use my hands."

"Did you stop? I mean, stop using your hands?"

"Yeah," she replied, flatly. The soft-spoken teen-ager's eyes appeared dull, expressionless.

"And what happened next?"

"He told me to take off my pants."

"And did you?"

"No. I didn't do anything, so he just pulled them off me. He told me to lay back on the seat, so my head was against the door, and then he took them off."

By now it was obvious to Shaw why the young girl's demeanor had troubled Detective Robinson. Beth had barely moved her hands from her lap, and she talked in an measured, even monotone. Her emotions seemed totally flat.

"OK, Beth," Shaw said, "now I want you to describe for me exactly the sexual acts he forced on you, in the sequence they happened, and how he forced you to comply. Are you OK with that?"

"Uh-huh," she answered quietly.

"OK, just tell me how it happened."

"After I was lying down, he started to rub me down there and then put his fingers in me."

"And how long did that go on?"

"A few minutes. And then he licked me."

"He performed cunnilingus on you?"

The young girl's faced reddened. She didn't know what the word meant.

"OK, now," Shaw continued, "I want you to describe any sexual dysfunction the man might have had."

Beth didn't know what that term meant, either.

"How did he function sexually?" Shaw said patiently. "By that, I mean, did he have an erection, or did he have difficulty getting or maintaining an erection? Did he have an erection when he pulled his shorts down, or did he have one later?"

Beth closed her eyes as if concentrating. "No," she said thoughtfully. "No, he had an erection as soon as he pulled down his shorts. But as soon as he pulled them down, stuff just came out of it."

"You mean he had a premature ejaculation?" Shaw asked.

"I'm not sure," she said. "Could you tell me what that means?"

"In other words," the detective explained, "he climaxed, but without touching his penis himself, or by having you touch it. In other words, it just happened by itself."

"Yeah."

"OK," Shaw said. "Now," what happened next?"

"Then he told me to put his thing in my mouth."

"Do you mean his penis?" Shaw asked.

"Uh huh."

"And did you comply?"

"Yeah."

"How long did that last?"

"Just a few minutes. Then he put me down in the seat and got on top of me and put his penis in me."

"How long did the intercourse last?"

"Maybe five minutes."

"OK, next I want you to tell me if he said anything when he was doing these things, starting with when he had you lie down in the seat and he took your pants and panties off."

Beth appeared to try very hard to concentrate. After a moment, she said, "When he was rubbing me with his fingers, he said, You have a nice pussy, but you probably already know that. And when he made me put his thing in my mouth, he kept saying things like kiss it, and lick it, and suck it."

"Did he say anything during the actual intercourse?"

"He kept telling me to kiss him on the mouth. He told me I'd better kiss him, because he said he was in control."

"He actually used the words *I'm in control* during the intercourse?"

"Uh-huh, he said it a couple of times."

"Did he say anything else you can remember?"

"He asked me if I was enjoying it."

"During the intercourse?"

"Yeah."

"Did he at any point demand that you say anything to him, to verbally respond to him in any way?"

"No."

"OK, did his attitude change? I mean, during the actual rape? Did he act differently at any point during the actual attack? What I mean is, what was the tone of voice he used, when he told you to do something? Was it matter-of-fact, or did he sound angry? What tone of voice did he use most of the time?"

"Sometimes it seemed like he was trying to be nice to me," Beth said. "But some of the time he was so mad I thought he was going to kill me."

"Did he attempt to conceal his identity in any way?"

"No," Beth said. "It didn't seem like it mattered, I

guess. But he did put my gloves on and use them to wipe off the car where he'd touched it."

"Did he take anything from you? Money, rings, jewelry, anything?"

"Just my gloves."

"How would you describe him? I mean, by the way he was dressed, his personal hygiene, that sort of thing. Was he neat, clean? What were his clothes like?"

"He had on blue jeans and a jean jacket. They were lived-in. They weren't new. But they seemed clean. It looked like they'd been ironed. He seemed clean."

"All right, Beth, I want to go back to something you told Detective Robinson. You said the man appeared to be intoxicated, or acted like he had been drinking. Why did you think that? Did you smell alcohol on his breath?"

"No, I didn't smell anything," Beth said. "Well, he smoked in the car, and I could smell smoke on his breath. But I don't think I smelled alcohol."

"What made you think he might have been intoxicated?"

"He couldn't seem to concentrate on the road," Beth said, growing slightly more animated. "He'd do OK for a while, then he'd kind of weave in and out of the lanes. And then he'd kinda catch himself and would drive OK for a while. It was almost like he'd be dreaming, then he would wake up and see where he was."

"So, he just sort of lost concentration from time to time and weaved in and out of the lanes. And that made you think he could have been drunk?"

"Yeah."

The man had weaved in and out of the lanes while looking for a place to rape the teenager. Then, in Beth's words, he'd "catch himself and drive OK." When he finally did find a place to stop, he had experienced a premature ejaculation. What Shaw had suspected from reading the report was now almost certain. The man must have been fantasizing, probably from the minute he had abducted the teenager or even before.

After a few more questions, Shaw asked Beth if she had received any phone calls or notes or knew of anything else that might indicate she had been targeted for the attack. Beth said she had not.

"OK," he said. "You've given me a lot of good information, Beth. Let's go out to your mother."

Escorting Beth to her mother, Shaw thanked them both for coming in on such short notice. He gave them his card and said he would call them within a day or two if the police needed further information. Then he went back to his office and sat down. He rewound the tape and replayed the interview.

Listening to the teenager's emotionally flat voice, Shaw now understood why Detective Robinson had found her demeanor unusual. But Shaw suspected that Beth's emotions were simply flat. What she had gone through had been so emotionally traumatizing that the youngster was simply dealing with it the only way she knew how.

Yet Shaw was convinced Beth was telling the truth. And he was equally sure Beth was not the first

victim of the man who had abducted and raped her.
He had known exactly how to control Beth, to a
point that she never tried to escape or resist. He had
used the gun to instill fear and had reinforced her
fear by saying that he had just robbed a jewelry
store. Then he had repeatedly reassured her that she
would be released unharmed. First he had used fear
to throw her off balance, then offered her a way out.
Seizing on the belief that she would be released,
Beth had not resisted or attempted to escape.

Equally disturbing, Shaw was almost now certain
the man had engaged in some kind of sexually violent fantasy. As he drove, he had probably been
totally lost in a fantasy of what he would do with the
teenager once he found a secluded place. The fantasy had been so strong that the man had experienced a premature ejaculation.

Shaw knew that most sexual predators experience strong sexual fantasies, usually beginning when
they are young children. In this man's mind, it was
likely that Beth's abduction and rape had been nothing more than a "date" that ended with sex. He had
picked up his date, gone parking, made her move
over next to him, kissed, and then had sex with her.

Shaw had no doubt the man was a control freak,
a dangerous sociopath who would do anything to
live out his fantasies. The next morning the report
was teletyped to every police and law enforcement
department in the nation, in the hope that somewhere an officer might recognize the offender's modus operandi.

Within hours, Shaw received a teletype from the

police department in Eugene, Oregon. A series of rapes had taken place in Eugene involving a man who matched the description Beth had given. Shaw phoned the officer assigned to the case. According to the officer, the offender in Oregon usually abducted his victims in shopping center parking lots. He used a small-caliber semiautomatic pistol during the abductions and appeared to be very familiar with the area around Eugene.

Could it be the same man? Shaw wondered as he hung up. Had the offender from Oregon been passing through on the interstate and simply stumbled upon Beth in the parking lot? This suspect appeared to have been unfamiliar with the streets and roads of Pocatello. That indicated he was either a visitor from out of town or perhaps someone new to the area.

9

Liz Smith worked in a collection agency in old-town Pocatello and lived in a small house on Main Street. Her husband had died just over a year ago. Now Liz shared her house with her daughter Tammy Retzloff and her son-in-law Martin. The household also included a large, blue-eyed malamute named Char, who usually wore a bright red handkerchief around his neck. The house, located in a working-class neighborhood of modest single-family homes, lay just west of the Union Pacific rail yards. It was the second house from the corner. Just inside the chain-link fence that surrounded the tiny front lawn grew a large elm tree. Liz Smith was washing dishes when the phone rang.

"Hello?"

"Elizabeth, you've got to come over to Dave's house and see this wall mural my cousin did," her friend Pearl said. "He's just moved up here from Louisiana, and he can really paint!"

Both Liz and her daughter Tammy had developed an interest in arts and crafts. Tammy, in her late twenties, suffered from hydrothorax, an illness that caused fluids to accumulate in her body. She was unable to work full-time. But when her health permitted, she enjoyed painting T-shirts and wooden knickknacks by hand. She sold a few to friends or gave them away as gifts. Like Dave Haggard, Tammy and her mother often scoured garage sales on weekends in search of things they could use around their house, especially craft supplies.

Liz drove to Haggard's home in Chubbuck. Haggard met her at the door and ushered her into the den. Pearl was there, along with her relative from Louisiana.

"This is my cousin, Jim Wood," Haggard said. Wood smiled and shook hands with Liz. Then Haggard stepped back from the wall so that Liz could have an unobstructed view of his new mural. "Well, what do you think of my wall?" Haggard asked.

A huge mountain scene covered the entire wall. The colors were vivid and the details precise. A placid lake in the foreground reflected tall green trees. A snow-capped mountain peak towered in the background. The rugged granite peak resembled the nearby Teton Range. Liz was impressed. "It's gorgeous."

"He did it from his head," Haggard explained as Liz took in the scene. "That rock in the lake there, he used a picture for that. Took a picture of a rock in the river up near Arco. But everything else is just from his head," Haggard said proudly, tapping his temple with his fingers.

James Wood stood quietly to the side, watching Liz admire his painting.

Liz's daughter Tammy met Wood a few days later when she and her husband visited Haggard. Not only was Wood a talented painter, she discovered, but also a self-taught tattoo artist.

"I've got a real ugly tattoo," Tammy said, tugging her T-shirt down in front to reveal a large tattoo of a butterfly above her left breast. "It's supposed to be a butterfly," she said, "but it looks more like a moth. Can you do anything about it?"

Wood studied the tattoo for a moment. He decided he could improve it by adding color. Tammy was delighted with the results. "He made my moth into a butterfly!"

Soon Wood, Liz, and Tammy developed a friendship. Martin, Tammy's husband, sometimes joined the three of them. They often went to the Pilot House to eat or held poker parties at Liz's house. But Martin never developed the friendship with Wood that his wife and mother-in-law did. "Martin doesn't trust Jim," Tammy told her mother. "He said he was 'too nice' to be real." But Wood continued to be a frequent guest at Liz Smith's small house on Main Street. Often, if there was a party, Jim stayed overnight, sleeping on the sofa in the living room.

Networking through Tammy and her mother, Wood began to cultivate other acquaintances around Pocatello. Word of his return to Idaho also quickly spread to his extended family on his mother's side. Like most people who met the soft-spoken newcomer from the South, his relatives found Wood polite and friendly. Wood was, from all outward appearances, a very likable person.

What the people of Pocatello didn't know was that Wood could never be their friend. He was *not* a likable person. He gave only the *appearance* of being their friend. As always, Wood was like a chameleon changing colors. He behaved the way he needed to at the time to take advantage of whomever he was around. Now, he behaved as a newcomer to town who was grateful to sell his paintings for some extra money. To onlookers, Wood appeared to be settling into a routine in Pocatello.

Even though he paid no rent for his room at Haggard's house, the income from his paintings was not enough. Wood took a job as a dishwasher at Tina's Ox Bow Inn, a restaurant and bar in a motel on Yellowstone Avenue, but Wood quit after about three weeks. Next, he found work with a builder in Pocatello, but he walked off the job after working less than two hours. But Wood's poor work record was not his only problem.

Even in rural Idaho, Wood could not leave his dark past behind. Rumors began to circulate among his extended family that "Jim" had served time in prison for "cutting up" two young girls. Some of his older relatives also remembered his troubled past in Idaho, which included three separate stays at the youth correctional center in St. Anthony. Wood freely admitted to having served time in prison in

Louisiana. But he rarely told the truth about why he had been sent to Angola, saying he had been in the penitentiary for "passing bad checks." The truth, of course, was quite different.

Shortly after he learned that Wood was living with Haggard in Pocatello, Earnest Arnold, Wood's half brother in Texas, wrote letters to several of his relatives in Idaho. In the letters, Arnold warned his relatives of his fears about his half brother, adding that if Wood "stayed in Idaho long enough," his concerns would be "proven right." Although Arnold wrote letters to several of his relatives warning them about Wood, he did not write Haggard.

Wood and his half brother Arnold had moved to Idaho with their mother, Hazel Godwin, shortly after her husband was sent to federal prison at Leavenworth. Arnold was her son from a previous marriage. When Hazel Godwin died in the fire at the potato processing plant in Rupert, Idaho, Arnold was sent to live with relatives in Texas. James, who was eight at the time, was adopted by his maternal aunt and uncle, Mildred and Gene Wood, and lived with them in Idaho Falls. Following the adoption, young James' last name was legally changed from Godwin to Wood. But Wood and his half brother had remained in touch over the years. Later, Arnold was one of the few visitors Wood received on a regular basis during both of his terms at the Louisiana State Penitentiary at Angola.

In 1985, when Wood was being considered for early release, Arnold, a former policeman, offered to provide Wood with a place to live. Wood was released from Angola the following year. Arnold was there to meet him. Together they drove back to Arnold's home in Texas, where he furnished Wood a room in his house and helped him find work. Wood eventually went to work as a truck driver for the carnival out of Tyler, Texas.

But the living arrangements soon soured, in large part because Arnold disapproved of Wood's relationship with a gay man named Jimmy Twiggs. Wood had met Twiggs while they were both imprisoned at Angola. In exchange for sex, Wood had protected Twiggs, his "bitch," from other inmates. Arnold insisted that the arrangement to have Wood live with him and "straighten out his life" failed in large part because Wood refused to end his relationship with Twiggs. The final straw came when Wood asked Arnold to allow Twiggs to move in with him. Arnold refused. Wood moved out. Arnold became convinced his half brother was beyond redemption. Hence his letters to relatives in Idaho warning them about Wood.

Two days after the abduction and rape of Beth Edwards, an article appeared on an inside page of the *Idaho State Journal*. Under the headline *"Man Abducts, Rapes Teen Saturday Afternoon,"* the article read, "Police were searching for a white male, about 38 years of age, 5 feet, 9 inches to 5 feet, 10 inches tall, with short brown hair, a goatee and a mustache. He was wearing blue jeans and a jeans-type jacket with a white fleece collar." The article ended with a request that anyone with information concerning the crime should call the Pocatello Police Department.

Along with the article was a computerized composite of the suspect. The stark black-and-white image showed a broad-faced man with a high forehead and a full mustache and goatee.

The story in the *Journal* did not go unnoticed by several of James Wood's relatives and new friends. Privately, some said the drawing resembled "Jim." The next day, Wood shaved his goatee, leaving only his mustache. Liz Smith noticed something else about Wood shortly after the story appeared in the newspaper: Wood suddenly stopped wearing one of his favorite jackets, the jean jacket with the fleece lining.

Within a day, the Pocatello Police Department received an anonymous tip concerning a possible suspect in the rape of Beth Edwards. The tip was passed on to detective Shaw. The caller, who refused to give a name, had suggested the police check out a "James" or "Jim" Woods, erroneously adding an *s* to the last name, who lived in Chubbuck. The caller felt "Woods" might be responsible for the rape that had been reported in the paper. The caller added there was a rumor floating "among the family" that "Woods" had served time in prison for rape and that he strongly resembled the composite sketch that appeared in the newspaper.

Shaw ordered a computer record search for a "Jim Woods" or "James Woods." The search turned up several people by that name in Pocatello, in Chubbuck, and across Idaho. Shaw collected photographs of those with criminal backgrounds and took them to the small apartment where Beth lived with her mother. Beth carefully studied each of the photographs, but none matched her vivid recollection of the man who had abducted and raped her. Furthermore, Wood had not registered his Ford Ranger in Idaho. A DMV records search, which would have shown a James "Wood," was negative. And because the caller had refused to give a name or phone number, police were unable to contact the person for additional information.

During the cold winter months, the sky was often gray, and a thick blanket of snow covered the Portneuf Valley. At Liz Smith's house, James Wood enjoyed flashing his wad of bills around at the parties and all-night poker games. On occasion, when her small living room was not sufficient for the number of people involved, the participants pooled their money and rented adjoining rooms at one of Pocatello's better motels, often the Holiday Inn near Interstate 15. The gleaming new motels, restaurants, and modern subdivisions in the foothills overlooking the area were a world away from the cramped neighborhood on Main Street where Liz Smith lived. But most of the parties took place in Liz's living room, often lasting until the early morning hours. They were smoky, boisterous affairs, with relatives and friends coming in and out. Sometimes the entire party moved to a cousin's home nearby.

On one such occasion, Tammy, her husband Martin, Wood, and several other friends were gathered in the living room of Liz's home for a game of poker. Later a relative of Tammy's, along with two young women, in their twenties, came to the door.

"Come here, darlin'," Wood smiled, waving one of the women over as they came inside. "Come over here and sit on my lap."

The woman, who had never met Wood, smiled but declined his offer.

"Look what I got," Wood said, taking out his wallet. He opened it and held up a handful of cash, waving it around for the woman to see. "Here," he said, holding the money out toward the woman. "You need some cash?"

Laughing, the woman slid down into his lap, playfully putting her arms around his shoulder.

Wood leaned forward and spread the money out on the coffee table. "Here, darlin'," he said, "You take that. It's all yours."

Everyone laughed when she reached over and took the money.

The next day, the young woman called Tammy. "I feel bad about taking his money," she said. She had taken over $100, and now she wanted to give it back. Tammy returned the money to Wood.

Later that same night, a side of Wood's personality that hid behind his facade reared its head for the first time among his new friends. Wood, Tammy, Martin, and three other men sat around the coffee table in the living room playing round after round of blackjack. Suddenly, Wood glared at Tammy, who was sitting on the floor.

"You fucking bitch!" he shouted, out of the blue.

Everyone was stunned into silence. Tammy had

no idea what she had said or done to cause Wood to call her a bitch. And from the look on his face and the tone of voice he had used, she knew he had meant it. Suddenly, Tammy's husband and two of the other men jumped to their feet, ready to fight Wood. Wood stood up and stormed out, slamming the door behind him.

Wood called Tammy the next day and apologized. "I was drunk," he said. "I must've been too drunk to know what I was saying."

Soon the incident was forgotten. Wood continued to visit Tammy and Liz. The parties went on much as they always had.

In reality, Wood was not drunk that night. For Wood to have become drunk would have meant a loss of *control*. Something had triggered his rage. For a brief moment, he had revealed his true, unpredictable nature.

10

Hemmed in on three sides by brooding mountains, Pocatello and the Portneuf Valley settled in for a year of near-record snowfall. As blizzard after blizzard stormed into the valley, the city's snowplows began their rounds in the bitterly cold predawn darkness.

The holidays came and went. The ski slopes were open at Inkom, a few miles south of the city limits near Portneuf Gap. In Pocatello, the city maintained cross-country ski trails in Ross Park. The rolling spaces of the city's public golf courses, too, were the sites of many improvised cross-country ski trails.

For Beth Edwards, life continued, although it was not the same, would never be the same. She immersed herself in schoolwork. Yet the memory of what had happened was never far from the front of her mind. At those times, when the memories emerged, the young teenager often retreated into her art, a source of contentment that had been a passion even before that day in November. Sketches and watercolor paintings covered the walls of her small bedroom. Some were whimsical, some were not.

Just as Beth Edwards sat at the kitchen table of her mother's small apartment, only a few miles away James Edward Wood sat working on paintings at the kitchen table of Dave Haggard's house.

For Detective Shaw, work settled into a familiar routine. He had been to Beth Edwards' apartment several times, each time taking with him new photographs of possible suspects for her to examine. None were of the man who had raped her. No new leads had emerged.

Wood, too, followed a now-familiar routine, stopping in for coffee at the Pilot House to chat with the owner, Annie, and her daughter Mitzi. In the evenings, he often had dinner with Liz Smith and Tammy Retzloff. He tried another job, this one with a construction company that erected metal buildings.

He was let go after three days.

But Wood continued to earn "spending" money with his paintings and occasionally by designing tattoos for Ty Chacon, the owner of a small tattoo shop on Yellowstone Avenue. The two had met when Wood briefly worked as a dishwasher at Tina's Ox Bow Inn. Their friendship had developed around their common interest in tattoos.

At first glance, Wood and the much younger

Chacon might appear to be unlikely friends. Chacon was stoutly built, with tattoos covering his back, chest, both arms, and hands. One of his large body tattoos featured the upturned beak of a swan, the image following the contour of his neck. Chacon wore his long, thick black hair pulled back in a ponytail. His skin was dark. So, too, were his eyes. He wore a thick black mustache. A silver loop hung from his left ear. In contrast, the, now clean shaven Wood was low-key and modest looking. But Wood appeared to enjoy Chacon's company and the atmosphere of the tattoo shop. Even when there was no work sketching designs for tattoos, Wood often stopped in to chat. Chacon's shop was in a small shopping center, a few doors down from the Subway sandwich shop.

"He loved Subway sandwiches," Chacon said. "Whenever he stopped at the Subway shop, he'd come in to my shop and say 'hello.' He told me he'd been in prison. But he was an older guy, and I just figured he was over that kind of thing. I figured that was in his past. But my wife couldn't stand the man. He'd come over and say, 'Hi. How're you doin'?' Things like that. And she'd just ignore him. I asked her why she didn't like him. She said he was just too nice, like it was an act. She thought he was creepy."

Chacon was most appreciative when Wood gave him one of his paintings. However, Chacon found the image rather haunting. It was a painting of an Aztec warrior in full ceremonial dress. In his arms he held the limp body of a dead girl, eyes closed, her head tilted back, her long hair flowing toward the ground. The dead girl, who was very young, was a sacrificial offering to the gods, Wood said.

A few minutes before eight on a bitterly cold evening in March, James Wood walked into the bright warmth of the Subway sandwich shop on Yellowstone Avenue. There were no other customers inside. In the back room, Jason Hatt, the only clerk on duty, heard the bell that meant a customer had walked in. The eighteen-year-old high school student greeted the customer. Wood was wearing a dark blue jacket and a blue baseball cap.

"Boy," said Wood, rubbing his hands together. "It's cold out there!"

"Yes, sir, it is," said Hatt.

"What've you got that's hot?" asked Wood, glancing up at the menu board. Before young Hatt could reply, Wood ordered a spicy Italian meatball sub. "And make sure it's real hot," he added.

Jason turned his back to the counter to put the sandwich in the microwave. When the teenager turned to the counter, he froze. Wood raised his left hand like a bandanna to hide the lower part of his face. In his other hand, Wood held the small silver semiautomatic. The small of the muzzle was pointed directly at the young teenager.

"Open the cash register and give me all the bills," Wood said with purpose.

Shaken, Jason walked along the counter toward the cash register.

"Don't reach under the counter," Wood said calmly, moving with Jason as he went toward the cash register. When the drawer slid open, the young man nervously began pulling out the bills.

"Now put them in a bag," Wood ordered once the boy had emptied the drawer.

"Yes, sir," Jason said. He stuffed the money into the bag and held it across the counter for Wood.

Wood took the money and walked to the open end of the counter. "Come on down here," he said.

Pale with fear, the young boy made his way to the end of the counter.

"Kneel down on the floor," Wood said, pointing with the muzzle of the pistol. *Oh, my God, is he going to shoot me?* the boy thought to himself. Shaking, he did as he was told and got to his knees behind the counter.

"Just stay there till I'm out," Wood said. Then he disappeared into the cold darkness.

A few seconds after he heard the door close, Jason Hatt, peering over the counter, cautiously rose to his feet. The parking lot outside was lit in the amber of the safety lights. There were one or two cars in the lot, but no sign of the man. Still trembling, Jason dialed 911.

Officer K. Linn of the Pocatello Police Department arrived shortly after other officers had set up a perimeter in the area of the Subway shop and had begun searching for anyone matching the description the young man had given. Officer Linn interviewed Janson, later writing in his report:

Mr. Hatt stated that at no time did the suspect seem in a hurry. He never seemed nervous, and was described by Mr. Hatt as being almost polite. Mr. Hatt estimates that the total time the suspect was in the store was approximately three minutes. Mr. Hatt did not see what direction he approached from or left in. The only other item that Mr. Hatt could remember about the suspect was that during the time he ordered the sandwich, he spoke in what he (Hatt) considered a normal tone and that during the robbery, he spoke in a slightly more quiet voice.

Later, young Jason went to the detective division at the police department, and worked with an officer to complete a Compusketch composite of the suspect. The next day, the sketch of a wide-faced man wearing a dark baseball cap appeared in the *Idaho State Journal.*

11

For Jeff Underwood, the recurrent dream had started when he was a young man, before his marriage to Joyce and the birth of their first child. It was always the same. In the dream, Jeff was the father of a young girl. The child was missing, so he began to search for her. It came to him that he should look near water. That water was a river—a wide, dark, swiftly moving river. Near the river he would find his daughter. In the dream he always was too late. His daughter was dead. When he saw what had happened to his daughter, the dream ended. It was always the same. He still had the dream from time to time, even after he was a married man with children.

When he was about to graduate from high school in Aberdeen, Idaho, Jeff Underwood did not know

what he wanted out of life. He considered joining
the U.S. Army. Instead, at the last minute, he decided
to attend Rick's College, a predominantly Mormon
college in Rexbury, Idaho. But on the summer evening in 1979 when he first met Joyce Browning, a shy,
pretty young woman with long auburn hair, he knew
exactly what he wanted. He wanted to marry her.

Jeff was a quiet, likable young man with a new-
found sense of confidence and purpose after returning from his mission in Virginia. There, for two
years, he had followed a disciplined routine, rising
each morning at 6:00 for an hour of personal study.
Dressed in dark slacks, a white shirt, and a tie, Jeff
then set out on long days of "tracting," spreading the
message of the Restored Gospel—The Book of Mormon—on behalf of the Church of Jesus Christ of
Latter-day Saints.

"I had an old blue bicycle I used in Virginia on
my mission, and it had an odometer on it," Jeff said.
"It was stolen just before my mission ended. The
odometer had over 5,000 miles on it."

Now that he had completed his mission, Jeff was
ready to fulfill another sacred tenant of the Mormon
faith—to marry and have children. After his first date
with Joyce at a dance sponsored by the Latter-day
Saints (LDS) in Pocatello, Jeff knew he had found the
woman with whom he would share that sacred duty.

Even though Joyce had agreed to go out with the
young man, she had no such strong feelings. Home
for the summer from Rick's College, Joyce attended
a family reunion a few weeks after meeting Jeff.
There, one of her aunts took her aside.

"Joyce, are you serious about that young man?" her aunt asked.

The question surprised Joyce. In truth, she had not given much thought to her feelings toward Jeff. "No, I don't think so," Joyce replied.

But young Jeff persisted. After returning from his mission in Virginia, Jeff re-enrolled at Rick's College. One weekend that fall, he offered to give Joyce a ride home to Pocatello. "It was about two hours out of my way, Jeff said of his journey, "But it was worth it just to get to see her."

Less than three weeks after telling her aunt she was not serious about the young man, Joyce and Jeff were engaged. On December 27, 1979, they were married at the LDS temple in Idaho Falls. After graduating from Rick's College in farm management, Jeff accepted a job with a welfare farm owned by the Latter-day Saints Church in Greeley, Colorado. The happy couple soon began fulfilling what they considered their duty to bring children into the world. In 1980 their son Jamen was born—the first of six children.

While living on the welfare farm in Greeley, the couple's second child was born, a daughter whom they named Jeralee. Five weeks premature, Jeralee weighed only four pounds nine ounces when her parents brought her home from the hospital. Perhaps for that reason, and because she was the couple's first daughter, little Jeralee held a special place in her mother's heart.

Almost from the time Joseph Smith founded the Mormon church in 1830, the faithful have been encouraged to keep daily journals both to record their lives and to serve as a record of family history. The study of genealogy is important in church doctrine because members are often "baptized for the dead" in the belief that their deceased ancestors can participate in their salvation. On September 5, 1982, Joyce wrote in her journal:

> Jeralee is almost eight months old, and she is doing so many things now that haven't been recorded. She has two teeth on the bottom, which she has had for probably a month. She has been scooting around and is now starting to crawl, which she does quite a bit of the time. This last week she started pulling herself up to things like the bookshelf and chairs. She has this thing with her tongue, where she tightens her bottom lip, then moves her tongue in and out, hitting her lip on the way out and making a popping, bubbly sound. I have been trying to stop nursing her, but she doesn't like the bottle, or maybe the goat's milk, too well. If I hold her like I would to nurse, then she is better at taking the bottle, perhaps out of a sense of security.
>
> This morning she said "momma, momma" between cries.

Two years later the family moved to Payson, Utah. But their family ties in Idaho were strong. In 1987, Jeff accepted a job as a custodian for several LDS chapels in Pocatello, and the young family moved back to Joyce's hometown. By the time the

Underwoods settled into their modest ranch-style house on a quiet cul-de-sac on the southwest side of Pocatello, their family had grown by three more girls: Jennifer, Janice, and Jessica. In 1991, the couple's sixth child, a boy named Justin, was born. Shortly before his birth, Jeralee was baptized and one day later was a confirmed member of the Church of Jesus Christ of Latter-day Saints.

In September 1992, ten-year-old Jeralee Underwood had a proposal she wanted her mother to hear. "Mom," she said. "Jamen and I have decided we want a paper route."

Joyce Underwood knew her daughter was strong-minded and independent. Still, she was surprised that Jeralee wanted to take on a newspaper route. Jamen was old enough to accept the responsibility, but Jeralee was a still a little girl who all too often had to be reminded to do her homework. Not only that, Jeralee had other obligations. She had begun dancing lessons when she was four, and now she was taking clogging lessons. She was also vice president of the student council at Indian Hills Elementary School and president of her primary class at church. Now she wanted to take on the added responsibility of a newspaper route?

"Are you sure?" Joyce said.

"Yes," Jeralee answered. She was sure.

"Why on earth do you want a paper route, Jeralee?" asked Joyce.

"I want to earn my own money," the freckle-faced youngster said, her large, round glasses making her look extra serious. Jeralee explained to her mother that she had a plan for the money she would earn. She would tithe—give 10 percent to—the church and open a savings account for the rest. Of course, she would keep a small amount for spending money.

The next day, Joyce drove Jeralee to the *Idaho State Journal* building near old-town Pocatello. After a brief interview with the circulation manager, Jeralee and her mother signed the paperwork. Ten-year-old Jeralee was told she had a job.

There was more good news. The route that included their own neighborhood was available. To Joyce's relief, that meant Jeralee and Jamen would never be more than nine or ten blocks from home. A truck from the printing plant would deliver the papers for the route to their door. On nice days, the two could deliver the papers on their bikes. If the snow was too deep for their bikes, the route was short enough for them to walk.

The circulation manager gave Jeralee a list of her customers, a collection book, and two canvas newspaper bags with the *Idaho State Journal* logo on the side. Also included was a short lecture on the importance of delivering the newspapers on time every day, regardless of the weather.

Jeralee and her brother began the route a few days later. Jeralee took half of the route, Jamen the other. Jeralee soon became a familiar sight along her route. She quickly developed a reputation for always taking care to place her papers on her customers' front steps or porches. Just as quickly, Jeralee discovered that collecting was her favorite part of the job. Often customers invited her into their living rooms and served her soft drinks. Jeralee relished the opportunity to sit and talk. She especially enjoyed visiting with her elderly customers.

That winter, the thought of her two young children going out into the predawn darkness on cold winter mornings was too much for Joyce to bear. On Sundays, she got up at 5:00 a.m. and helped her children load the heavy newspapers into the family's blue Chevrolet station wagon. Maneuvering over the icy roads, she drove them along their route.

12

Spring came slowly to Pocatello in 1993. At last, the days grew longer. Storms moved in from the west less frequently. The dull gray sagebrush began to turn green. At higher elevations, juniper trees took on a fresh green hue that signaled the arrival of a new season.

James Wood was introduced to Brenda Davis, a single mother of three. Although Wood only days earlier had asked Tammy Retzloff if she knew any-one he could "go out with," Wood met Brenda purely by chance. She and two of her children, a pretty eleven-year-old named Erika and Erika's young brother, were visiting a mutual friend of Tammy's when Tammy and Wood arrived for drinks. Although it would be several days before Wood and Davis went out together, Wood made it a point to establish a friendship with her two children from the moment he saw them.

"How would you two like to come out to the country and ride four-wheelers?" Wood asked the children later that evening.

"Yes!" both replied enthusiastically.

"Well, we'll have to ask your mama if it's OK," Wood said. "Why don't you ask her if you can spend the night with me out in the country? We can get up early and go riding in the morning."

Although their mother had never met Wood before, she gave her children permission to spend the night at Dave Haggard's house. Wood drove the two children home with him when he left later that evening. When it was time for them to go to bed, Wood gave the children separate bedrooms upstairs. After they were tucked in, Wood went downstairs to his bedroom.

Later that night as she lay in bed, Erika heard a soft knock at her bedroom door. Then the door opened. In the dim glow of a night-light, the eleven-year-old saw Wood come into the room. He closed the door quietly and sat down on the edge of the bed.

"Scoot over," he whispered.

The little girl did as she was told. Wood slipped into the bed beside her. She felt his hand near her hip. Suddenly, Wood pulled down the sweatpants she had worn to bed. He leaned over and kissed her on the buttocks.

"No!" she screamed. "Stop that!"

Wood drew back, aware her scream might

awaken the others in the house. Erika jumped out of the bed. She ran down the hallway to her brother's bedroom, closing the door behind her. She slept with her brother the rest of the night.

When Wood saw Erika and her brother the next morning, he was friendly and pleasant, as if nothing had happened. But Erika was quiet and withdrawn and remained that way until later in the morning, when Wood led the two children out to the garage where Haggard kept his four-wheeler. At first, Wood let each of the children ride in his lap as he steered the four-wheeler around the yard, the children squealing with delight. Then, after showing them how use the throttle and brakes, Erika and her brother took turns racing the noisy four-wheeler around the yard and into the pasture behind the house. But even though the excitement of riding the four-wheeler had brought the little girl out of her withdrawn mood, she made a point to never again be alone with Wood.

Little Erika kept her secret about "Jim," the man her mother was dating. She never told her mother or her fourteen-year-old sister Karen.

One beautiful Saturday, James Wood borrowed Dave Haggard's custom van and invited Karen and her mother to go for a ride. The three of them spent the afternoon driving through the foothills above Pocatello, enjoying the view of the valley below and the snowcapped mountains in the distance. Brenda invited Wood to a party that night at a friend's house. On the way, Wood dropped Karen off at home while he and her mother went to the party. Later that night, after Karen had gone to bed, there was a knock at the door. It was Wood.

"You're mama's real drunk, and she won't come home," Wood said. "Can you come with me and help me talk some sense into her?"

Karen, dressed in the sweats she had worn to bed, went out into the night and got in the van with Wood.

"I think a friend took your mom out to the Holiday Inn for something else to drink," Wood said as he started the van. They drove through town and took Pocatello Creek Road. Karen saw the lights of the Holiday Inn as they neared the interstate. But Wood didn't stop. Instead, he turned around and started back toward town. They traveled along a small road near the campus of Idaho State University, heading up into the eastern foothills.

"I think my friend must've taken your mama out to his house," Wood said as the big van climbed a steep grade into the darkened hills. Now the lights of the city were below them. Wood turned onto a narrow asphalt road, then drove down a dirt road leading through a pasture. When the headlights caught a place where the hard-packed road widened, Wood pulled the van to the side and stopped. He switched off the lights and turned off the ignition.

"I thought his house was up this way," Wood said. "Guess I must've took a wrong turn somewhere."

He turned toward Karen. She looked at him with

questioning eyes. Suddenly, he grabbed her by her long hair. Moving between the front seats, Wood dragged Karen to the back of the van and threw her on the carpeted floor.

"Do what I tell you, or I'll blow your fucking head off!" he said.

He pulled off her sweatpants and panties.

"Now," he said, standing over her, "we're gonna fuck!"

When he finished, Wood glared at Karen. "I'll kill your mother if you ever tell anybody about this," he warned. Then he drove the terrified young girl down from the foothills and dropped her off in front of her house. Like her younger sister, Karen would not tell what "Jim" had done— until one day in June much later.

James Wood continued to visit the Pilot House Restaurant that spring, usually stopping by in the afternoon to chat with Annie or Mitzi and to check on the sales of his paintings. On weekday afternoons after school, Mitzi's young son Scott was usually there, too, sitting quietly at a table drawing or practicing his letters on a notepad. Scott usually stayed at the restaurant until just before the dinner rush, when his mother took him home.

Wood and Scott had become pals. The young boy clearly enjoyed Wood's company. Wood seemed to have a way with the boy, as he usually did with young children. Mitzi saw nothing sinister in the fact that Wood had taken such an interest in her young son. Besides, as a single parent who put in long hours at the restaurant, she thought it was probably good for her son to have a man to talk to occasionally. Scott was interested in fishing and the outdoors. Wood also loved to fish. Scott listened with rapt attention as Wood spun entertaining tales about the fish he had caught and the places he had fished.

Since the beginning of spring, Wood had brought a companion with him on his visits to the Pilot House. Wood had introduced his friend as "Gary," a stout, muscular man built like the weight lifter he was. Soon, Gary also took an interest in Scott. Gary told the six-year-old intriguing stories, one of them about how he had won a weight-lifting championship when he was in prison.

"The next time I come back," Gary told young Scott, "I'll bring you a surprise."

A few days later, a beaming Wood walked in. Gary followed close behind him. In Gary's thick arms was a huge golden trophy that stood over four feet tall. On it was an engraving that read First Place, Bench Press, 1992 Pacific Northwest Power Lifting Competition. Gary placed the trophy on the counter in front of young Scott, whose eyes danced with excitement.

"Here," he said proudly. "It's yours!" Although Mitzi did not discourage Scott from talking to Wood's friend, she grew concerned when she learned Gary had served time in the state prison in Boise.

It was not long after his friend gave Scott the trophy that Wood and Gary stopped in at the Pilot House for the last time.

"Gary and I wanted to know if we could take Scott to the drag races," Wood said.

Mitzi was surprised. As far as she could remember, Wood had never said anything about having an interest in drag races. It also struck her as odd because Scott was not even at the restaurant. Scott's grandmother Annie had taken him home earlier.

"I don't think so," she replied.

"Why not?" Wood asked. Suddenly, the friendly, self-effacing man seemed demanding.

"Well, for one thing, I hardly know you," Mitzi said. "I know I've seen you a lot, but I don't really know you. I'm not letting my son go off at night with somebody I don't know."

Wood's eyes hardened. "Well, fine," he said coldly. He turned and stormed out the door.

Gary, his muscular friend, had been watching from the waiting area. Across the crowded dining room, Mitzi saw Gary glare at her, then turn and follow on Wood's heels. Wood didn't look back. Neither he nor his friend came back to the Pilot House again.

13

The drive from Pocatello to Salt Lake City on Interstate-15 takes roughly three hours. About thirty minutes into Utah, the Wasatch Range appears, its snowcapped spine running parallel to the interstate. Further south, as the sprawl of Salt Lake City begins, traffic becomes heavy. The open farmland gives way to a string of towns, their names reflecting the region's Mormon heritage: Ogden, Brigham City, Wood's Cross, Kaysville, Bountiful, and finally Salt Lake City proper.

As spring slipped into summer, James Wood acquired a more reliable form of transportation. With his pickup on its last legs, he worked out a deal with Dave Haggard for a four-door 1984 Buick Century. Mechanically, the car was in good condition. For a nine-year-old car, the mid-sized Buick looked good, too. It had a dark-brown vinyl roof over a light-tan body and chrome-wire wheel covers with narrow-banded whitewalls.

"His old Ford Ranger was just about shot," Haggard said. "So I got him the Buick. Paid him $500 for his truck, then turned around and got him the car. I had the title put in his name so he'd have to get insurance. But I don't know that he ever did. I sold it to him for $1,900. He'd only paid me $300. That's all he ever paid."

Wood liked the car because it was very average looking—nothing flashy that might draw attention to him. Within days of getting the Buick, he was on his way to Salt Lake City. About 10 P.M., he left the interstate and parked in the parking lot of a high-rise office building in Wood's Cross, Utah. Wearing a black Los Angeles Raiders T-shirt outside his jeans and a dark blue baseball cap, Wood locked the car and walked from the high-rise to a nearby Sizzler steak house. Inside, he placed a take-out order for a child's portion of the chicken dinner.

"It's for my son," he said to the young girl behind the counter. Taking his receipt, he moved down to the cashier's station to pay. There, another teenage girl rang up his total. With tax, it came to $2.13. Wood reached into the pocket of his jeans and placed two one-dollar bills next to the cash register.

"I think I've got change," he said, digging into his side pocket. He took a half-dollar from among several coins in his pocket and handed it to the cashier.

"I don't know where to put this," the cashier laughed, holding the silver coin up to examine it as the cash drawer slid open. There were no compartments in the cash drawer for half-dollars.

"Put it all right here," Wood demanded, lifting his left hand just above the counter so that the cashier could see the .22 pistol he now held.

The sixteen-year-old cashier stepped back, puzzled. "What?" she asked.

"Shhh," Wood said. "Be quiet!" Then he reached into the open cash drawer with his right hand and began taking fives, tens and twenties. When he had taken all the money he could hold in one hand, Wood turned and strode down the hallway and out the main entrance. Wood's routine was so smooth, other employees working near the counter never noticed that a robbery was taking place.

Wood drove off with over $1,050. From the parking lot of the Allstate Building where he had left his Buick, he drove south toward Salt Lake City. He turned onto State Street and soon found himself in a seedy part of the city known for its aggressive street-walkers who flag down business from men cruising by in cars. As Wood came to a stop at an intersection, a young blonde in a tight miniskirt and a blue sweater leaned toward him and motioned for him to roll down the window.

"What color's your money?" she asked, leaning close to the window to look at Wood.

"I've got money," Wood said.

"Well, that's good," she smiled. She opened the door and got in the car with Wood.

"I've got a room at a motel," she said, nodding in

the direction Wood's car was facing. "Just go on down this street."

Suddenly Wood floored the Buick, the engine straining as the car accelerated. At the next intersection, he cut sharply and sped around the corner, then raced down the darkened street. Ahead, he could see a green-and-white freeway sign marking an entrance ramp.

"Slow down, honey," the woman said, glancing back, then at Wood. "My friend's gotta follow us!"

Steering with one hand, Wood reached behind him, pulled the small silver pistol from his back pocket, and held it in his lap. "Just sit still or I'll blow your fuckin' head off!" he shouted.

The woman froze, her face white with fear. Wood moved the pistol to the seat between his leg and the door. Under the glow of streetlights, the Buick sped up the ramp and onto Interstate-15, merging into the light late-night traffic.

"Please, mister," she pleaded, just take me back, I promise I won't do anything, I won't tell anybody. Oh, fuck, mister, please just take me back where you got me!"

"Shut the fuck up!" Wood exclaimed. The darkened foothills of the Wasatch Range were on his right. From the climb of the lights, he knew he was heading into the mountains, where he could find an isolated spot. Leaving the interstate at the next exit, Wood pulled onto a narrow dead-end road. With the lights of the city spread out below them, Wood forced the terrified woman to perform oral sex on him. Then he raped her.

When he finished, Wood pulled his pants up. "Show me how to get to that motel you were talking about," he said flatly.

Following her directions, he drove back to State Street. As they drove, she pointed out the bright neon sign of a motel in the distance. He stopped the car on the street in front of the motel.

"Just walk away from the car and don't look back," he said. The woman jumped out of the car. Wood watched her for a moment as she hurried toward the motel, her high heels clicking on the sidewalk.

The next afternoon, Tammy Retzloff answered the phone that rang at Liz Smith's house. It was Wood, calling to apologize. Tammy's birthday was the day before. He had missed it.

"I'm sorry I wasn't here for your birthday," Wood said. "But I had to drive down to Salt Lake City yesterday." To make it appear that he was making up for not being there, Wood said, he would like to treat everybody to dinner tonight. Tammy's husband, too, if he was not working.

It was typical of Wood, she thought. He was always loose with his money. He was always taking people out to eat. One day he had money, the next day he was broke.

That evening, Wood drove Tammy and Liz to Mama Inez's, a Mexican restaurant and bar on Yellowstone Avenue. In the past, if Wood had been in the mood for Mexican food, they would have gone to the Pilot House. "I think they're closed on Sunday," he explained.

When they were finished and the waitress brought the tab, Wood picked it up and glanced at it, then reached in his pants pocket. He paid the tab, which came to around $30.

Jim had a *roll* of money, Tammy noticed. Then, to her astonishment, he left the waitress a $30 tip! "Lord, you made that gal's day!" she laughed.

A few days later, James Wood walked into Papa Paul's Café and sat down at a booth near the glass entrance. Just across the parking lot from the Phillips 66 truck stop, Papa Paul's was a favorite with truckers traveling Interstate-15 and Pocatello locals as well. Wood was dressed casually, wearing a dark blue jogging outfit and a pair of scruffy white Reeboks. A waitress took her order pad from her apron and went to the booth to take his order.

"I'll have the Nitetime Omelet," Wood said, placing the menu back in its rack. "I'll take coffee with that."

She smelled beer on the man's breath.

The waitress nodded and scribbled down his order. It was almost closing time, and she was eager to leave. "Make sure you get that straight, now," Wood said, half smiling.

Other than Wood, there were only five or six customers in the café. One by one, the others paid their tabs and left. It was past closing time now. Each time someone left, Wood watched as Matt Warren, the manager, walked the customer to the entrance and locked the glass door. He left his keys in the door.

When Wood finished eating about ten minutes later, he was the only customer left. Taking one last sip of coffee, Wood got up from the booth and went to the cashier's stand. He handed his check and a twenty-dollar bill to the waitress behind the cash register.

"I enjoyed it," Wood said, as she handed him his change. He put the money in his front pants pocket.

"Just a second, and I'll let you out," said Matt walking ahead of Wood to the door. He stood back and held the door open for Wood. But Wood hesitated. Then Wood reached into his jogging pants and produced the small silver pistol. "Lock the door and leave the keys in it," Wood said, waving the pistol at the manager's stomach.

Matt did as he was told. As Matt started back inside, Wood pushed him forward, toward the cashier's stand. The waitress looked up from counting the money and saw the strange look on the manager's face. She knew immediately they were being robbed. She felt weak, almost nauseous.

"Put the bills in a sack," Wood ordered. "Then bring it to the back."

Her hands trembling, the waitress took the bills out of the cash drawer and stuffed them into a take-out bag.

"Get the rest of the crew out here," Wood insisted. Matt called out, "Everybody come on out here and do like he says."

When all five employees were in front of the cash register, Wood lined them up, single file. "Don't nobody make any sudden moves!" Wood said loudly. He ordered the manager to tell the other four employees they were to move to the office. "And tell them they better not try anything," he added, holding the barrel of the pistol to the manager's side.

"All right, now," Matt said. "Everybody go on back to the office and do what you're told." The manager realized that Wood must have known the safe was in the office.

When the cook reached the office door, he tried to turn the doorknob, but it wouldn't open. The door was locked.

"Open it," Wood said.

"The keys are on the ring you made me leave in the door," Matt replied.

"Well, shit!" said Wood. Still guiding the manager by the back of his shirt, Wood turned everyone around and made them walk single file back out to the front foyer. "Get the keys out of the door and lock it," Wood directed.

Once again, Wood lined everyone up and marched them back to the office. "Now open the damn door," Wood said. Matt opened the door, and Wood guided him over to the safe. He ordered everyone else to lie down on the floor.

"You've got the combo, now open it!" Wood snapped. "And you've got two minutes to do it." As Matt started spinning the dial on the safe, Wood looked back at the four employees lying on the floor. One of the waitresses was crying. "Don't cry, darlin'," Wood said softly. Then he looked over at the cook. "You, cook," Wood said. "Crawl on over here."

"Put your arms up!" Wood ordered, once the young man had crawled over in front of him. Lying on his stomach, the cook put his arms up and behind him. As he did, Wood reached into the front pouch of his jacket and took out three lengths of thin white rope. Then Wood pulled the cook's hands behind his back and tied his wrists. Next, he pulled the cook's feet up and tied them together, then ran the extra rope through the bindings on the cook's hand. The young man was hog-tied. "Don't worry," Wood said as he checked the rope for tightness. "Somebody'll find you sooner or later."

Meanwhile, the manager was having trouble getting the safe open. Matt was so nervous he kept spinning past the combination. Wood glanced over and saw that he was still fumbling with the dial.

"Get the goddamned safe open now!" Wood yelled, "or it'll be all over!"

Taking the second length of rope in his hands, Wood ordered the dishwasher to crawl over to where he stood. As Wood started tying the dishwasher's hands, Matt at last got the safe open. Wood, tying the dishwasher's hands, had his back to the manager.

Matt locked eyes with one of the waitresses. He took the key ring and found the key to the front door. Holding the key up for the waitress to see, he nodded toward the office door. *I'm going to run*, he silently mouthed. With that, the manager was up and through the open office door, running for his life. Matt bolted through the dining room to the outside door, jammed the key into the lock, pushed the door open, and sprinted across the parking lot toward the lights of the Phillips 66 truck stop.

Matt had escaped so quickly that a few seconds elapsed before Wood realized he was gone. Without a word, Wood made a dash for the door and ran out into the night.

14

uesday, June 29, 1993. It was late afternoon. Joyce Underwood stooped over Jeralee Underwood's bicycle, trying her best to repair a loose wheel. Jeralee wanted to do her collecting before the Fourth of July weekend because her family had made plans to go out of town. Joyce struggled to tighten the axle nut with a pair of pliers, but they kept slipping off the nut. Already her hands were black with grease, and her forehead beaded with sweat.

"Mom, is it ready yet?" Jeralee called from the front door.

"Not yet," Joyce replied. She looked up and saw Jeralee toting her canvas newspaper bag over her shoulder. "Honey, I don't think I'm going to get this fixed before you need to leave."

"That's OK, Mom. I'll just walk." It was a beautiful

summer day. "Bye," Jeralee said, as she started down the sidewalk. Her thick auburn hair spilled out of the opening in the back of her Utah Jazz basketball cap. At the end of the driveway, Jeralee looked back over her shoulder at her mother, still wrestling with the bicycle. "I'll be back in a little while," Jeralee assured her mother.

"Bye," Joyce said. She paused and watched her daughter walk around the corner and disappear from sight.

James Wood arrived early at Liz Smith's house that evening. Tammy Retzloff had called and invited him for dinner. She had planned to cook a roast with mushroom gravy. Wood, relaxing on the sofa, was chatting with Liz Smith's six-year-old granddaughter when the doorbell rang. Char the malamute ran toward the door and began to bark.

"I'll get it," said Liz as she made her away across the thick brown living room carpet toward the door. She opened the door and saw their newspaper carrier, Jeralee Underwood, standing on the small stoop. "Hello, Jeralee," Liz said.

"Hi. I'm here to collect for the paper."

"Well, young lady, you're a little early, aren't you?" Liz Smith smiled, looking at Jeralee over her glasses.

"Yes ma'am," Jeralee replied. "I just thought I'd get it done before the weekend."

"Come on in," Liz said, holding the screen door open. As Jeralee stepped inside the small foyer,

Wood turned to look at her. He smiled. "So, you've got your own paper route?"

"Yes, sir."

"You must be a smart little girl. Why, it wouldn't surprise me if you didn't grow up to be president some day!"

Jeralee looked skeptically toward Wood, then rolled her eyes.

"Here you go," said Liz, handing Jeralee the check.

"Thanks," Jeralee said. She folded the check and slipped it into her canvas bank bag.

"Bye-bye, now," Liz said, watching Jeralee leave through the gate in the chain-link fence. Jeralee strolled down the sidewalk toward the house of Blanche Tucker, her next customer on the route.

Wood stood up, looking out the small living room window. From where he stood, he could see Jeralee walking up the steps of the house.

"I've gotta run to the store," Wood announced. "I forgot to get beer."

"Well, you'd better hurry back," Tammy said from the kitchen. "Dinner will be ready soon."

"I want to go, too!" Smith's granddaughter said.

"Not this time, sweet," Wood said, patting the little girl on the head. "Not this time."

Wood walked outside and looked toward the house Jeralee had just entered. She was still inside. He hurried to his Buick and turned down the street that ran along the side of the house. He made a sharp U-turn, parked on the opposite side of the street, and waited. Jeralee would have to walk directly in front of his car when she crossed the street.

Inside Blanche Tucker's house, Jeralee Underwood waited politely as Blanche went to get her purse.

"Here you go, dear," Blanche said, paying Jeralee in cash.

"Thank you," Jeralee said as she handed Blanche a receipt.

Blanche opened the door and watched Jeralee bound down the sidewalk. Then she happened to catch another glimpse of the young girl, coming into view through one of Blanche's large picture windows. She was crossing the street. Blanche noticed Jeralee was heading toward a man in a dark cap standing beside the open door of his car. Blanche did not recognize him. Because of the shadows cast by the overhanging elm trees, she could not make out his face. Now Jeralee was talking to the man.

"I'm glad I caught up with you," a smiling James Wood said to Jeralee Underwood. "You know that check Mrs. Smith gave you? Well, she's worried it might not clear the bank. She wanted me to see if I could catch you and give you cash instead of the check."

"OK," Jeralee said.

Jeralee stopped and unzipped the canvas bank bag. She found the check Liz Smith had given her and handed it to the man.

"Have you got change for a twenty?" Wood said, holding out a twenty-dollar bill.

"I think so," Jeralee said. She looked back into the bank bag, thumbing through the bills. As she began to count out the change, Wood moved closer to her. Then, in one quick movement, he grabbed her by the back of her neck and forced her head down. Wood turned her toward the car and literally threw the little girl into the waiting Buick.

"Get down and stay down!" Wood yelled, pushing hard on the back of her head. He gunned the Buick through the intersection.

Jammed against the firewall, Jeralee felt the car race ahead. Almost immediately, she felt the car slow down. Just as suddenly, she was slung back in the other direction as the car accelerated again and veered sharply to the left.

Now the car was traveling along a relatively straight path, picking up speed. Had Jeralee been able to look out the window as the car sped down Bannock Highway, she would have seen the backyard of her own house not a hundred feet away, where her father was weeding peas in the garden.

15

Blanche Tucker gasped. What should she do? From the window of her home at the corner of Carter and Main Streets, she had witnessed what looked like an abduction. She had seen Jeralee Underwood unzip her bank bag and take something out—it appeared to be a small piece of paper—and hold it out to a man. What had happened next occurred so quickly and so unexpectedly that Blanche wondered if she had actually seen it. The man had reached out and pushed Jeralee into the car. Then the car pulled away and headed directly across Main Street and continued down West Carter Street. Blanche had watched as the car sped down Carter Street and disappeared from view.

She rushed to the phone and called Jeralee's parents, but the line was busy. She dialed the number again. Still busy.

Concerned, Blanche called Jeanne Johnson, a friend who lived in the same subdivision as the Underwoods. When Jeanne answered, Blanche told her she thought that she had seen Jeralee being pushed into a car by a man she had never seen before. "I'm worried about Jeralee," Blanche said. She asked Jeanne to run to the Underwood's house to tell Jeralee's parents what she had seen.

Jeanne Johnson hung up the phone and hurried to the cul-de-sac where the Underwoods lived. Jeanne knocked on their front door. Joyce Underwood, who had just gotten off the phone, came to the door. Upon hearing of the incident, Joyce tried to stay calm as she dialed Blanche.

"Did Jeralee have anyone helping her with her paper route today?" Blanche asked.

"No, she didn't," Joyce replied.

"Well," Blanche said, "I saw Jeralee getting in a car I haven't seen in the neighborhood, and I was concerned. It looked like she was pushed into the car."

Joyce knew it was not unusual for people who knew Jeralee to see her near the end of her route and offer her a ride home. Maybe that was the case. But something felt very wrong. A look of panic overcame Joyce's face. She ran to the back door and called to her husband. "Something might've happened to Jeralee!"

Jeff Underwood dropped his dusty gardening hoe and ran to the back door. Frantically, Joyce told him what Blanche had seen.

Taking Jeff's truck, the Underwoods rushed

through the neighborhood, scanning both sides of the street, looking for any sign of Jeralee. Jeff pulled in at the Little Stinker convenience store and stopped at the pay phone on the side of the building. His hands trembling as he held the phone, Jeff told the police officer who took the call that his eleven-year-old daughter had possibly been kidnapped. From the sound of Jeff's voice, the officer sensed the seriousness of the call and asked Jeff where his daughter had last been seen. "At Main and West Carter," Jeff said.

Within minutes of Jeff's call, logged at 6:43 P.M. on June 29, 1993, Detectives Joe Kingsley and Rick Capell of the Pocatello Police Department were dispatched to the corner of Main and Carter Streets. Arriving in separate cars, they met Jeff and Joyce in front of Blanche's house.

When the detectives asked Blanche to describe the car she had seen, she said it was a large, later-model car, possibly light gray or light blue in color.

"It was hard to tell exactly," she said, because the car was parked under the shade of the big tree on the corner. Yet she believed the car was about the same size and shape as a neighbor's car, a 1987 Oldsmobile Cutlass. The man was white, appeared to be clean shaven, and had a stocky build. Although she could not be sure because of the distance, she guessed he was between thirty and forty years old. Blanche told the detectives that as best she could recall, the man wore a dark-colored shirt, possibly plaid, and a dark-colored hat. Exactly what kind of hat the man wore Blanche was not certain.

Detective Capell asked Blanche if she would be able to identify the man if she saw him again. Blanche was unable to see the man's face clearly, she said, so she was not certain she could identify him. Blanche also recalled that although she had seen Jeralee being pushed into the car, she could not see the little girl as the car drove away.

The detectives immediately contacted the shift commander, Lieutenant George Housel. A description of the car, the driver, and Jeralee was radioed to every officer on the streets as well as to the Bannock County Sheriff's Department and the local office of the Idaho State Police.

Meanwhile, Detectives Capell and Kingsley decided to drive south on Arthur Street in hopes of spotting the car. They realized that when a child is abducted, the abductor usually goes to the first secluded location he can find and molests the child. South Arthur Street offered many such locations. Several side roads led into the isolated foothills and south to the Mink Creek Recreation Area. The wilderness area offered scores of secluded trailheads and parking areas where a car could not be seen from the main roads.

It was almost dark now. Capell and Kingsley knew their chances of finding Jeralee lessened with each passing minute. In separate cars, they drove several miles south, each trying different side roads and turnoffs. But neither detective saw any sign of the car or anyone matching Blanche's description of the abductor. They returned to the city limits just after dark.

One of the first telephone calls Jeff made when he and Joyce returned from Blanche's house was to an elder in their ward of the Church of Jesus Christ of Latter-day Saints. Mormon wards are similar to parishes in the Catholic Church, usually consisting of roughly 600 members. Within minutes of Jeff's call, an organization within his ward set up to deal with personal emergencies went into action.

Ward members and friends flocked to the Underwood's home, many bringing covered dishes. Among the first to arrive was Larry Wilson, who took charge of an organized effort to help find Jeralee. Search parties were organized. Members of other Pocatello wards arrived to take part as well. Still others began an orchestrated campaign to contact local and regional media outlets, including the *Idaho State Journal*, the television stations in Pocatello and Idaho Falls, and all radio stations broadcasting in southeastern Idaho. Faxes were sent describing Jeralee and the clothes she was last seen wearing as well as Blanche's description of the abductor's car. That evening, the first news of Jeralee's abduction was broadcast on the late local news by both local TV stations, KPVI and KIDK, plus KIFI in Idaho Falls.

Working throughout the night at a printing company owned by a "brother," ward members printed thousands of posters and began to distribute them throughout Pocatello and the region early the next morning. Copies of the posters were faxed to all truck stops west of the Missouri River.

With a large headline that read "Missing," the posters pictured Jeralee and gave a description of the suspect and his car. A reward was offered for Jeralee's safe return.

16

In the past fifteen years, five young girls had been abducted and murdered in Pocatello. They ranged in age from twelve to fourteen. Four of their bodies had been found in or near Pocatello. One had been found in the foothills east of town. Two others had been found east of Malad, Idaho, a small farming community in the mountains forty-five minutes south of Pocatello.

Only one case was cleared, that of Lynette Dawn Culver, more than a decade after the twelve-year-old's mysterious disappearance from Pocatello's Alameda Junior High School. While awaiting execution in Florida, serial murderer Ted Bundy had confessed to her killing. However, her body was never recovered.

Against the backdrop of four unsolved kidnapping and murder cases—all involving young girls—

alarm bells went off throughout the Pocatello Police Department. Moments after the dispatch on Jeralee Underwood had gone out to the officers on the street, Chief of Police James Benham was called at home and told of what was now assumed to be an abduction of an eleven-year-old newspaper carrier.

Benham immediately drove to Main and Carter Streets to take personal charge of the investigation, ordering a door-to-door canvas of all homes in the vicinity. He directed officers to search the three locations around Pocatello where the bodies of the murdered young girls had been found. The sheriff of Oneida County was asked to conduct a search near Malad, where the other remains had been found. Killers often become territorial. If the same person responsible for any of the four unsolved killings was involved in Jeralee's abduction, it was possible he might return to one of his same "dumping grounds."

Adding to Chief Benham's gut-wrenching anxiety was the fact that at least thirty minutes had elapsed between the time Blanche Tucker had seen Jeralee being pushed into the car and the time the police received the call from Jeff Underwood.

When Scott Shaw got the call on the Underwood abduction, he was on the first day of his long-awaited vacation. His wife Vonny was going to finish out the rest of the week at the *Idaho State Journal*, where she worked in advertising sales. Then, on Saturday, they were taking their daughter Krissy and son Jason to Disneyland.

The shift commander had given Shaw the facts of the case as they were known, over the phone. "OK, thanks. I'll check in first thing in the morning," Shaw said. Shaw looked at his watch. It was nine-thirty. Almost four hours had passed since the apparent abduction had taken place. *Either she'll be safe at home by tomorrow morning,* Shaw thought, *or we'll be looking for a body.*

As Shaw walked back into the den and sat down, Vonny glanced up at him. She did not ask what the call had been about, nor did the children. Nothing was said about the vacation. After Shaw went to bed later that night, he would not see his family, except when they were sleeping, for over a week.

Dave Haggard was up early that next morning, sitting at the kitchen table having his morning cigarette and coffee, when he heard James Wood's Buick drive up. He watched through the blinds as Wood got out of the car and took a plastic bucket out of the trunk. He uncoiled a garden hose from the side of the house, filled the bucket with water, hosed down the car, and washed it. When he finished, he pulled the car into the garage. Haggard heard the sound of his wet-dry vacuum coming from the garage. A few minutes later the sound died, and he heard the Buick's engine start. He saw Wood back the Buick out, then drive around the garage and disappear from view. A minute or so later, Wood came in.

"You look like you've been up all night, Jimmy," Haggard said.

"I met up with some Mexican friends of mine,

and we ended up staying up all night," Wood said, heading downstairs toward his room.

When Haggard went outside later that morning, he noticed Wood had not parked his Buick in the driveway. Instead, he had pulled it into the pasture behind the house and parked it between Haggard's camper and boat. The camper and trailer hid Wood's Buick from the road. Later that day, when Haggard saw his cousin again, he noticed Wood had shaved his mustache.

The next morning, Scott Shaw woke up early. He looked at the red digital readout of the alarm clock on the nightstand beside his bed. It was almost five-thirty. He got up and called the morning shift commander.

Late last night, another witness had been found. Around 11:00, Ron Phipps, who lived near Blanche Tucker, had called Detective Joe Kingsley. Phipps said he called because his landlady told him Jeralee was missing. Phipps said he had been working in his yard earlier that afternoon, when he saw Jeralee talking to a man outside a car parked on West Carter. Phipps said he turned away for a moment, but the sound of a car leaving at a high speed caused him to turn around and look again. Phipps said the car "sped" through the intersection of Main and Carter Streets. At the end of the next block, the car turned left onto Arthur Street. Phipps said he saw the driver, but he did not see Jeralee. Although Phipps was not able to offer anything new about the appearance of the man, he did provide a better description of the car. It was a newer-model, cream-colored car with a dark vinyl roof. He believed the car was a Buick.

Shaw showered and got dressed, then drove to the corner of Main and Carter Streets, where the Underwood girl had been abducted. He was familiar with the location. He drove past the intersection every morning on his way to work.

Shaw parked his Ford Bronco facing north against the curb on Main Street. In the still morning air, he walked along the sidewalk in front of Blanche's house on the corner and went across Carter Street. Lieutenant George Housel had said the suspect's car was parked on the north side of Carter Street, a few feet back from the intersection with Main Street, when Jeralee Underwood was abducted. Shaw stopped under the heavy canopy of the big elm tree and looked back toward Blanche's house on the corner. The picture window on the side of her house looked directly out onto Carter Street. The window was no more than fifty or sixty feet from where the car had been parked.

Shaw knelt down and studied the place near the curb where the car had been parked. There were oil stains on the side of the street where other cars had been parked. There was a patch of loose gravel and fine sand near the intersection. There were tire marks in the loose gravel, but by now it was impossible to know if they had been left by the suspect's car or other cars that had passed by later.

Although the loose gravel would have made it

difficult to get a cast impression of a tire tread, it might still be possible to get a wheelbase measurement. That, at least, would tell police whether to look for a full-sized or mid-sized car. If they could determine the size of the car, a mid-sized car for example, police could request the vehicle identification numbers of all cream-colored, mid-sized General Motors cars in the state from the DMV. Knowing the size of the car could prove to be a crucial piece of evidence.

Looking east on Carter Street, Shaw could see a brush-covered barrier where the narrow street dead-ended less than a block away. Still, there were houses in every direction. It was a highly visible place to abduct a little girl, especially in broad daylight, at a time when traffic would have been fairly heavy on Main Street, with people passing through the neighborhood on their way home from work.

It was almost seven when Shaw drove back to the police station. No one who saw him that morning asked Shaw why he was not on vacation. He picked up a copy of the offense report by detectives Kingsley and Capell and went to his office.

17

It had now been almost fourteen hours since Jeralee Underwood disappeared. Six or seven officers, all outranking Shaw, gathered in Chief of Police James Benham's office. Various theories regarding the young girl's abduction were put forward. Some, such as the "runaway theory" involving a boyfriend or trouble at home, were immediately dismissed. That Jeralee was seen being forced into a car made it clear they were dealing with an abduction by a stranger.

Shaw, ill at ease in such meetings, said nothing. Listening to the conversation, he mentally rehearsed how he would answer if Behham or one of Shaw's supervisors asked his opinion.

From behind his large oil-finished desk, Benham focused and refocused the conversation, asking questions, occasionally interjecting his own opinions.

A tall, trim man in excellent physical shape, Benham had worked his way up from patrolman to chief. He had a hands-on approach to command and a reputation for putting the welfare of the men and women under his command above most anything else.

As Shaw continued to listen in silence, the conversation turned to a phone call Benham and Captain Lynn Harris had made to the FBI's Behavioral Science Center in Quantico, Virginia, earlier that morning. They had spoken with an expert in criminal profiling. Based on the information Benham and Harris had been able to provide at the time, the FBI profiler had offered a theory about the type of offender who had abducted the young newspaper carrier.

The offender probably had an "organized personality" and had carefully planned and executed the abduction. He was most likely a serial offender, probably someone who didn't live in or near Pocatello. To lessen the chances of being recognized, the offender usually traveled extensively to locate his victims. Generally, he chose locations that were high-risk for his victim and low-risk for himself— places where the abduction was unlikely to be witnessed. Following a successful abduction, the offender usually transported his victims as far away as possible before sexually assaulting them. He typically disposed of his victims in remote areas, making it unlikely their bodies would soon be found, if at all.

The officers continued to discuss the FBI profiler's theory. Then the topic shifted to what steps should be taken to find the man who had abducted Jeralee, someone who by now—if the FBI's theory was correct—could be two states away in any direction. Shaw remained quiet until Benham turned to him during a break in the conversation.

"What do you think, Scott?" the chief asked.

Shaw took a deep breath. He was about to contradict the FBI's theory, one theory that most of the officers in the room seemed to agree with.

"I think it's wrong," Shaw said. "I don't think he's an organized offender. I think what he did was very *dis*organized. Look at where it happened. Main and Carter, in broad daylight. There's heavy traffic in that area at that time of the day. Any number of people could have seen it, and two people did. I don't think it was planned at all. I think the prick just saw an opportunity and took it. And the witness said the little girl wasn't anxious or nervous when she was talking to him. I think that means it was somebody she knew, or at least somebody she'd seen before. Somebody in the neighborhood, or at least somebody who spends time there. I think he's local."

"Are you saying the Behavioral Science Center is wrong?" one of the officers asked Shaw.

"I'm saying I think there's a good chance that whoever took that little girl is still around," Shaw said.

No one spoke for a moment. Then Benham looked at Shaw. "OK, Scott, you're going to lead the case," he said. Benham made it clear that he wanted the case "locked down, coordinated, and focused." Turning to the other officers, Benham instructed that

Shaw, as lead investigator, was to have the full co-operation of every officer under the chief's command and that all of the department's resources were to be at the disposal of the investigation into the disappearance of Jeralee.

Before the meeting ended, the officers focused on other details of the investigation, including how to deal with the media. In less than fourteen hours, the case had already generated an incredible amount of media interest, in part due to the efforts of the Latter-day Saints. It was agreed that the police department would fully cooperate with the media. In fact, the police would seek the media's help in publicizing certain aspects of the investigation. The more coverage the case received, the more information they could expect to glean from the public. In a somewhat unusual move, the police agreed that Shaw's name and position as lead investigator would be made public. Sometimes, especially on high-profile cases like a child abduction, offenders had been known to make a game out of trying to match wits with the officer in charge of a criminal investigation. If that was the case, the man might attempt to contact Shaw and perhaps might be tricked into exposing himself. Shaw was to give as many press interviews as his schedule would permit.

When the meeting broke up a few minutes later, Shaw went back to his office. His first task was to organize the flood of information such a highly publicized case was likely to generate. Already, calls were coming in from other law enforcement agencies that had seen the teletypes and wanted to share information on similar cases. The police department even received calls from individual officers, some several states away, offering to come to Pocatello at their own expense to help in the investigation in any way they could, even if it meant simply answering the telephones.

Calls were coming in from the public, too, offering information on suspects or possible sightings of Jeralee or cars matching the description that had been reported on the local news. But the calls received so far were only the tip of the iceberg. If the fate of the little girl remained a mystery for any length of time, the resulting press coverage would generate an avalanche of calls from the public and with it the potential to devour both the time and energy of the manpower available to the investigation.

With that in mind, Shaw designed a tip sheet to be used by everyone answering the phones. It required personnel taking calls to record specific information, including each caller's name and number. Shaw would personally review all of the tip sheets.

Shaw was planning the investigation of Jeralee Underwood's abduction based upon two assumptions. First, investigators were looking for a body and for the man who murdered the little girl. By treating the case early on as a homicide, nothing would likely be missed if the young girl were found alive. But if Jeralee had been murdered, as Shaw suspected, then approaching every piece of evidence or potential crime scene as a homicide would preserve crucial evidence that might otherwise be lost. For that very reason, Shaw was intensely concerned about the massive public searches of the foothills and remote areas south of Arthur Street that had already begun. He knew the motives behind the search parties, organized by the Latter-day Saints and other civic groups, were well intended. Still, the news reports over the next few days showing hundreds of people searching through the tall, dry grass in the foothills and along the interstates, some swinging sling blades or probing with wooden poles, caused Shaw to cringe. He could not shake the image of scores of well-meaning citizens trampling across a fragile crime scene, destroying crucial evidence in the process.

Shaw's second assumption was that the man who abducted Jeralee was probably someone living in or near Pocatello. Therefore, the major focus of the investigation would be local. Lower priority would be given to distant and out-of-state sightings, although no reports would be dismissed out of hand.

Later that same evening, Shaw outlined the boundaries of what would be the largest door-to-door canvass in the history of the Pocatello Police Department. Sitting at his desk with a city map before him, Shaw marked the area to be covered, using Blanche Tucker's house as a starting point. The final canvass area encompassed more than a square mile, most of which was fairly densely populated. Every person living or working within the boundaries would be contacted. A system of cross-checks was devised to make sure anyone missed on the first round would be contacted on a second, and, if necessary, a third round. Next, Shaw drafted a contact sheet to be used by the officers conducting the canvass. In addition to any tips about the case, the sheets required the officers to list the names of everyone living in a household or employed at a business as well as the name of anyone who might have been visiting at or near the time Jeralee disappeared.

Wednesday, June 30, 1992. Warm, dry winds whipped through the Portneuf Valley. Just before ten that morning, Shaw left the station and drove to the home of Jeff and Joyce Underwood. Although Shaw had never met the Underwoods, he was familiar with the subdivision where they lived. Not only did he drive past it every day on his way to work, but a few years earlier, he had owned a home there. As Shaw turned into the subdivision of modest ranch-style homes and saw his old house, he was surprised by how close his family had once lived to the Underwoods. They lived on a cul-de-sac directly behind the house he had owned. It was obvious which of the three small homes belonged to the Underwoods. Two middle-aged women, carrying casserole dishes covered with aluminum foil, were walking toward the front door. Several cars were parked in front.

Walking up to the door, Shaw saw a girl's blue bicycle leaning against the front steps. Colorful plastic toys were scattered on the lawn near the driveway. But the children they belonged to were nowhere in sight. Shaw rang the doorbell. A well-dressed woman in her mid-thirties opened the door.

Behind her, Shaw could see several people talking in the small living room.

"I'm from the Pocatello Police Department," Shaw said. "I'd like to speak to Mr. and Mrs. Underwood."

The woman turned and led Shaw through the living room into a small foyer near the kitchen.

The tired, anguished looks on their faces left little doubt that the couple before him were the Underwoods. Joyce's dark eyes met Shaw's. Strain was etched into her face. Her eyes were red. Standing by her side was Jeff, a stubble of beard on his face, wearing the same dark blue work clothes he had worn the day before. Still, both husband and wife managed weak smiles as they greeted the tall detective.

"I'm Detective Scott Shaw, and I've been assigned to investigate your daughter's case," he said, first shaking Jeff's hand, then Joyce's. He could not help thinking how small and frail they both appeared. "Is there a place we can talk?"

"Maybe in the kitchen," Joyce said, her voice barely audible. She gestured toward the back of the house.

As Shaw followed the Underwoods into their kitchen, he glanced around the small house. It had the look and feel of a place where children lived. It seemed to him a loving home, too. Everywhere he looked, there were family photographs. On the upright piano in the living room was a framed photograph of Jeff and Joyce and their six children. At the top of the picture frame was the word *love* in bright letters. On the wall above the basement stairwell, he saw color studio portraits of Jeff and Joyce. Surrounding them were dark-framed portraits of each of their six children, arranged in order of their age. The portrait of a smiling Jeralee was just below Jamen, her older brother.

Every countertop in the kitchen was covered with casserole dishes, trays, and plastic containers of food. Those that did not fit on the counters covered most of the wooden picnic table that served as the Underwoods' dining table. Joyce pushed some of the dishes aside so that Shaw could have a place for his notebook. Shaw pulled out one of the wooden benches and sat down. The Underwoods sat across from him. Jeff took his wife's hand.

"What I need is for you to tell me everything you can about Jeralee, beginning with the clothes she was wearing yesterday," Shaw requested.

As Shaw took notes, Joyce described Jeralee's purple Utah Jazz basketball cap, her gray Utah Jazz T-shirt with purple trim, her large glasses with brown, semi-transparent frames. Her voice broke and her lower lip trembled. She bit down on her lip until she regained her composure.

Shaw asked the couple to describe their daughter—her personality, her likes, her dislikes. He explained that the information he collected would be sent to the FBI's Behavioral Science Center in Quantico, Virginia, and entered into the agency's Violent Criminal Apprehension Program (VICAP) computer system. The information on Jeralee would be entered into the computer system, which would scan the facts related to Jeralee's case and match them against similar crimes in the United States and Canada.

As he listened to the Underwoods talk lovingly about their daughter, it was clear Jeralee was a very responsible girl for her age. Both parents described her very mature attitude and demeanor. She required little discipline from her parents. Jeralee baby-sat her younger brother and sisters and helped prepare family meals. She always made friends quickly, they said. Jeralee enjoyed reading, drawing, and playing with her friends.

"Did she ever mention any kind of trouble with anyone on her paper route?" Shaw asked.

No, her parents said. She had never mentioned anything negative about anyone she saw or dealt with on her route. She already knew many of her subscribers before starting the route because most were neighbors and friends.

"Does she know about basic child safety?" Shaw asked.

Jeff said that she did. In fact, both he and Joyce had discussed it with her the day she started the route.

"We told her to never accept rides with anybody she didn't know," Jeff said, "or from people she knew but didn't feel comfortable with."

They had often stressed to Jeralee, and to all their children, to never walk up to a car if someone stopped them for directions or for any other reason. At Indian Hills Elementary, where Jeralee went to school, courses in personal safety were a part of the curriculum. The Underwoods added that Jeralee knew certain phone numbers to call if ever there was a problem and that she had always come straight home after delivering papers and collecting. Jeralee had a level of common sense, they said, that was far above her age level.

Shaw asked if Jeralee had received any phone calls that she had voiced concerns about or if the household had received any hang-up calls recently. Both Jeff and Joyce were adamant that she had not. Both parents stressed that if anything—no matter how small—were bothering Jeralee, she would have discussed it with them. Even if something minor was bothering her, they would have noticed a change in her behavior. Jeralee was always a happy-go-lucky child and very spirited.

Before leaving, Shaw cautioned Jeff and Joyce Underwood about phone calls they were likely to receive. The couple, sitting across from him, their hands still clutched together on the table, listened sadly as Shaw told them not to be surprised if they received crank calls. But no matter how cruel or upsetting, they should not change their phone number. There was always a chance Jeralee might try to call.

"People are going to be calling and claiming they've seen Jeralee," he warned them. False sightings were simply a part of such a tragedy. "I don't want you to get your hopes up or let somebody mislead you," he said, telling them to keep in mind that "99 percent" of the rumors and other information they were likely to hear would be false. "Unless the information comes from me," Shaw said, "assume it has no merit." Shaw could almost see their hearts sink. He asked that they keep a log of every phone call they received. Shaw also had the Underwoods sign a release giving the police permission to install a phone tap so that all incoming calls could be instantly traced.

Then Shaw discussed the media. The Underwoods told him they were already receiving some calls. He assured them the number of requests for interviews would increase as time went by if Jeralee was still missing.

"I want you to give as many interviews as you feel you're up to," Shaw said, stressing that it was extremely important that they make public pleas for Jeralee's safe return. "When you are interviewed, especially on TV, I want you to always have a photo of Jeralee," he said. Shaw recommended the Underwoods also display personal items like clothing or toys that belonged to their daughter. "There's always a chance that the person who has Jeralee might see it," he said. "If they do, personalizing Jeralee might make her a 'somebody' rather than a 'something' to him."

Shaw glanced at his list of topics to cover with the Underwoods. There were only two or three items left, and Shaw knew they would be the most difficult. "I'll need a copy of Jeralee's birth certificate," Shaw said, "and I'll need her medical and dental records."

Again, Joyce's lip began to quiver. Her shy eyes reddened. Jeff put his arm around her shoulder, and she fought back the tears, then got up to get the phone numbers of Jeralee's doctor and dentist. She would have to look for the birth certificate.

"I'll have someone from the station call this afternoon," Shaw said. "They can pick it up then."

Shaw looked at his watch. He had been at the table with the Underwoods for almost an hour. He wrote his home number on the back of his business card and gave it to Joyce, telling them that he would be in contact with them as often as possible and that they were free to call him at any time, day or night, if they needed anything.

Jeff held out his hand and thanked Shaw. His eyes rimmed in red, he assured Shaw that his family would receive whatever material and emotional support they needed from their church. "And from our Heavenly Father," he added softly.

Leaving the Underwoods' home, Shaw glanced at the house where he and his family had once lived. It was only two houses away. Perhaps it was the realization that his own family had lived so close to the Underwoods, that their children had grown up in the same neighborhood, done the same things, maybe even played together, that caused an overwhelming sensation of sadness to overcome Shaw. It could have been his own daughter, who was only one year older than Jeralee.

Later that afternoon, Shaw and Agent Richard McDaniel of the FBI office in Pocatello placed another conference call to the FBI's Behavioral Science Center. After discussing the case in detail with FBI experts, a limited criminal profile was agreed upon:

The offender is a non-specific sexual offender.

He feels he is inadequate and has a very low

self-esteem. He is a loner, with no close friends. He would be described as quiet, and perhaps strange or unusual. He practices poor personal hygiene and probably dresses in a casual manner, and would not wear clothes that are currently in style. He may also have some physical deformity, such as a limp or birthmark. He will feel very frustrated because of prior failures.

Late that evening, Shaw drafted a more detailed profile, one that would be used as a benchmark in evaluating possible suspects, tips, and other information, including contact sheets from the canvass. The profile was dated June 30. It read in part:

The offender is believed to be disorganized and therefore the actual offense had a probability that it was committed as a result of a compulsive act rather than an act well planned...The second point of consideration would be the ruse the offender used to have Underwood walk to an area or very close proximity to the offender and his vehicle. A witness reported that Underwood was showing something from inside her bank bag to the offender. This tends to negate a more common ruse, such as the offender displaying a police badge or assuming some other position of authority. The witness described Underwood as being totally without apprehension during their contact and this would further lend credence to the ruse being some type of trick designed to place Underwood in a position of something she is comfortable with. Under the circumstances, it is highly probable that the most likely ruse that would have a high level of success would be something dealing with what she was doing at the time of contact, which was collecting for her paper route. The degree of probability is rather high that the ruse would include a problem with a very recently collected payment. This could include a question of an unsigned check, overpayment, or something similar in nature. Based on this theory, it is reasonable to assume that the offender either paid for his bill or was present when a bill was paid.

Shaw added probable physical traits of the offender to the earlier profile. Shaw wrote, "statistically the offender will be somewhat 'pear shaped,' or have a 'beer belly.' He will probably drive an older-model car. The offender will statistically reside with a relative because he has no steady income."

Just after ten the next morning, Detective Mike Brennan began knocking on doors in Blanche Tucker's neighborhood. Although every household in the vicinity would be contacted later as part of the canvass, Brennan had a different goal. Working from a list of Jeralee's subscribers, he called everyone on the list and asked them if Jeralee had been to their house to collect on the day she disappeared. If she had, Brennan wanted to know if Jeralee had been paid by cash or check. He took account and check numbers from those who had paid by check, then notified their banks to place alerts on the checks in case anyone attempted to cash them.

When Detective Brennan got to Liz Smith's house, Tammy Retzloff came to the door. She told him that Jeralee had stopped by and that her mother had written her a check. Although her mother was at work, Tammy told the detective that she could find her mother's checkbook. Tammy went inside, then came back to the door with Liz's checkbook in her hand. She opened it to the postings and found the entry. The check, dated June 29, had been made out to Jeralee in the amount of nine dollars and was drawn on First Security Bank. Brennan wrote down the account number, the date, and the check number and later notified First Security Bank to place an alert on the check.

That same morning another officer drove the second eyewitness, Ron Phipps, around town and asked him to point out cars that most resembled the one he had seen leaving Carter and Main. He pointed out two, both off-white, early 1980s Pontiac Grand Prix.

That afternoon, the *Idaho State Journal* ran a banner headline: "Search continues for abducted girl." Below, a color photo of Jeralee showed her smiling, wearing her large, oval-shaped glasses. On the TV news that evening, both local network affiliates and another in nearby Idaho Falls led with the story of Jeralee's disappearance. Pocatello's Channel 3 featured an interview with Ben Smith, circulation director of the *Idaho State* Journal and ended with a close-up of the paper's afternoon edition with Jeralee's picture. "A somber mood has taken over the newsroom at the *Journal*," the TV reporter said. "Smith says today the *Journal* is missing a family member."

Another segment opened with video taken across Main Street, looking toward Blanche's house. The off-screen TV reporter began, "Neighbors along the 700 block of South Main where Jeralee was abducted yesterday are expressing their concern, as well." The video, shot in bright sunlight, showed the front of Blanche's house with blue sky overhead, the strong summer winds whipping through the dark leaves of the elms in front. To the right of Blanche's house was the blue-framed house of her next-door neighbor Liz Smith.

The news report shifted to a close-up of a resident of the neighborhood. "She's been our papergirl for quite some time," a woman with a plump face and long, straight, dark hair said. "She's just a really sweet little girl, and she's quite vibrant, you know. We're all real worried about her."

Inside the auditorium of the Pocatello Stake Center of the Church of Jesus Christ of Latter-day Saints, huge paintings with golden frames—some more than eight feet high—hang from the walls. The paintings depict images held in reverence by the faithful. In one, a young Joseph Smith kneels in prayer.

In one of the largest paintings—perhaps the most haunting—a pioneer woman leads a team of oxen pulling a Conestoga wagon across the prairie. As if the painting was a photograph, the woman seems to lead the wagon directly toward the lens of the camera. She wears a bonnet and a long, dark dress. Her face is grim. Her eyes look straight ahead as if fixed on the distant Salt Lake Valley, which Brigham Young had promised his followers would be a paradise on earth, a place where the enemies of the Mormons could not pursue the faithful. The woman's stride, frozen in time, is determined, as though she finds strength in the knowledge that each step westward takes her further from the persecution that had followed the Mormons ever since the prophet Joseph Smith revealed his visions of angels and the words of the golden plates. Alone in the driver's seat of the huge covered wagon is a child, perhaps two years of age. Like the mother leading the team of oxen, the child also gazes ahead. And riding close to the side of the wagon is a ghostly apparition, a wispy image of a knight in armor on horseback. It is the woman's guardian angel.

At 6:00 on Wednesday evening, the day after Jeralee had disappeared, a prayer meeting was held at the Pocatello Stake Center to pray for Jeralee's safe return. The Stake Center served as a chapel for three of the seven Pocatello wards. Although the prayer service had been hastily arranged, the remarkable organizational skills of the Latter-day Saints were evident as more than 1,000 members and others in the community filled the chapel to overflowing capacity. Members of the Mormon Church had fasted all day and offered prayers for Jeralee.

On the table next to a framed picture of Jeralee, thick stacks of "MISSING" posters, printed the night before, were now available. Church volunteers passed out the posters. On a wooden table at the front of the chapel stood another framed photo of Jeralee. Sitting next to it was a huge white teddy bear with a red ribbon around its neck. The teddy bear was one of Jeralee's favorite toys. Behind the pulpit stood dazed and sorrowful Jeff and Joyce Underwood, holding onto each other for support.

As the service began, Pocatello Stake Center President Kert Howard lifted his arms and asked the audience to join him in a hymn, "Sweet Hour of Prayer." The rich sound of the pipe organ filled the chapel. When the hymn was finished, Howard asked the audience to kneel in prayer. In a fluid movement, the crowd knelt. Hundreds lowered their heads.

"We are asking for a miracle," Howard began, his own voice breaking with emotion. "And we pray for guardian angels to surround Jeralee and protect her mind and body from harm."

Near the end of the service, Jeff moved tentatively to the pulpit. He feared public speaking, but now a strange calm had come over him as he gazed across the sea of faces before him. His voice thick with emotion, he looked out over the congregation and thanked the members of his church and everyone in the community for their support for his family and for Jeralee. Then he spoke directly to the man who had taken his daughter.

"Please don't hurt her," Jeff pleaded. "Please let her go. Let her come back to the family and friends who love her."

Outside, as the last rays of the sun cast a golden glow on the brick buildings of old-town Pocatello, Scott Shaw stood discreetly at the edge of the Stake Center's green, rolling lawn, watching the hundreds of people as they left. He had watched the same people arrive and had walked among the hundreds of cars that filled the center's three parking lots. He had written down the tag numbers of every vehicle even remotely resembling the car described by Blanche Tucker and Ron Phipps.

Beginning at 3:20 that same afternoon, traffic was stopped at checkpoints set up at intersections on Main Street, Arthur Street, and further south on the Old Bannock Highway. Staffed by officers of the Pocatello Police Department and the Bannock County Sheriff's Department, the traffic stops soon began to back up evening commuter traffic.

Officers handed out flyers with Jeralee's photo, a description of the man who had abducted her, and a description of the man's car. They asked drivers and passengers if they had been in the neighborhood yesterday afternoon. If so, had they seen Jeralee or a man driving a two-tone, early 1980s car? There was also a slim hope that a car and driver matching the description might be stopped. In the end, however, the checkpoints resulted in nothing more than delays for people on their way home from work or running errands.

Other officers and detectives were conducting a

canvass of all of the households on Jeralee's route. Among the questions they asked: Was anyone visiting your home yesterday? Do you know anyone who drives an early 1980s tan-or cream-colored car with a darker roof? No one, including those in Liz Smith's household, knew of anyone who drove such a car. No one reported that anyone had been visiting yesterday afternoon. Later, Liz would say that when police asked her if anyone had visited her home on the afternoon Jeralee disappeared, she told them "no" because, "We considered Jimmy like family."

It was almost two o'clock in the morning when Shaw finally left the police station and drove home for a few hours of sleep. As he climbed the stairs at home, he saw a note lying at the top of the stairwell. The handwriting of his twelve-year-old daughter read: "Daddy, please find Jeralee. I went to school with her and knew her. She was just one grade behind me. I love you, Krissy."

18

Thursday morning, July 1. Detective Scott Shaw arrived at his office in the detective division before six. Waiting for him on his desk were more than a dozen messages from police departments and agencies across the country. Several dealt with cases involving young girls who delivered newspapers and had been abducted under circumstances similar to Jeralee's. There were also at least a hundred tip sheets. Most named someone the caller believed might have been involved in Jeralee's disappearance.

Shaw began reading. He mentally compared the suspects listed in the tip sheets with the profile he had drafted. After reviewing each tip sheet, Shaw placed it on one of two stacks on his desk. The stack on the left was reserved for those he felt did not warrant action, at least for the time being. The stack on the right was the "promising" stack. Each of these would be checked out. Four leads in the "promising" stack all named the same person as a suspect: Tommy Ford. Apparently, all of the calls had come from regulars at the Friendship Club, a small bar about two blocks from the corner where Jeralee had been abducted.

One caller was sure Ford had been in prison for child molestation. That caller also said Ford matched the general description of the abductor he had heard in the news reports. Moreover, the caller said he had personally heard Ford talk about having sex with children, "something about needing to 'break them in right,' " he added. The other three callers said essentially the same thing: Ford was "weird" and a "pervert." One claimed Ford had followed Jeralee out of the Friendship Club on the day she disappeared. Another thought it suspicious that Ford had not been seen the day Jeralee disappeared. None of the callers knew where Ford lived.

Shaw read the sheets mentioning Ford over again. He found it hard to believe Jeralee had been inside the Friendship Club that day. Her actions had been accounted for from the time she left home until the time she was seen being shoved into the car. Nonetheless, he decided to have someone run a computer check on Tommy Ford.

While waiting for the results of the computer check, Shaw began returning calls from the other law enforcement agencies. There were no solid suspects in any of the abductions the other agencies had mentioned. The only case that appeared to closely match Jeralee's had occurred in Allentown, Pennsylvania. But that crime had happened very close to the time of Jeralee's disappearance. It would have been virtually impossible for the same person to have abducted both girls. Besides, Shaw was convinced that whoever abducted Jeralee had been in Pocatello for at least several days before she disappeared.

A short time later, Shaw received the results of the computer search on a Tommy Ford with a Pocatello address. The physical descriptions the callers had given seemed to match, but there was nothing in his background that indicated he had ever been arrested or sentenced for a sexual offense. But a DMV check had turned up a driver's license and a car registration.

Since there had been four calls concerning Ford, Shaw decided the man was still worth checking out. After going to the address that turned up on the computer check, Shaw learned that Ford had separated from his wife and had moved out. But Ford's estranged wife offered what Shaw considered an "interesting" bit of information. Asked for Ford's current address, his estranged wife said Ford was staying in a tent "somewhere on Pocatello Creek Road."

Later that morning, Shaw left the station and drove out Pocatello Creek Road, past neighborhoods of new housing and into the eastern foothills. There, among the juniper trees, he saw a KOA campground. The campground was filled with RVs and campers. Shaw turned into the small drive leading into the campground, looking for Ford's car. As he

James Wood
shortly after his
arrest in Pocatello,
on Tuesday,
July 6, 1993.

Foothills surrounding Pocatello, Idaho. Wood often drove into
remote area of the foothills where he would assault his victims.
Terry Adams.

Dave Haggard's home in Chubbuck, Idaho, where Wood lived from November, 1992, until his arrest eight months later. *Terry Adams.*

Painting on a saw by James Wood. He earned money selling paintings he did on old saws he'd found at garage sales. *Terry Adams.*

James Wood's Buick Century, parked in the pasture behind Dave Haggard's house. *Scott Shaw.*

Jeralee Underwood, age 10, school photo, 1992.

Jeralee Underwood, in costume, for school program, Young at Art Dance, 1992.

The Underwood family, Pocatello, November, 1992. *Courtesy of Underwood family.*

Jeralee Underwood, January, 1993, after she'd won a trip to Yellow Stone National Park for selling newspaper subscriptions.

The home of Jeff and Joyce Underwood, Pocatello, 1992. *Terry Adams.*

The corner of Main and Carter Streets in Pocatello, where James Wood abducted Jeralee Underwood on Tuesday, June 29, 1993. *Scott Shaw.*

Detective Scott Shaw, Pocatello Police Department, was the lead investigator on the Underwood case.

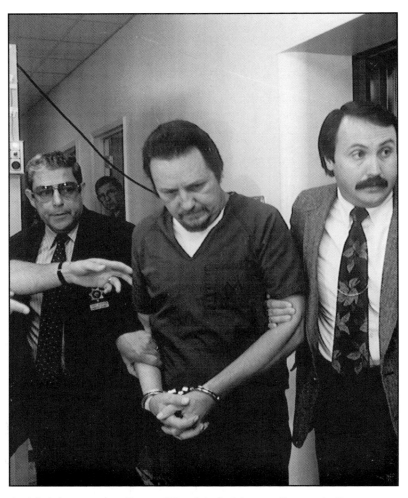

Amid tight security, James Wood is led into a Bannock County Court room, where he stood trial for the slaying of Jeralee Underwood. Wood is flanked by Ruben Robell, left, and Bannock County Sheriff Captain Jerry Hickman, right. *Doug Lindley, Idaho State Journal.*

Near Idaho Falls, divers search the Snake River for the remains of Jeralee Underwood. *Doug Lindley, Idaho State Journal.*

Pocatello residents Brain Prokschl, left, and Ty Friend, express their outrage toward James Wood. The two demonstrate, with a sign and noose, near the courthouse where Wood was arraigned after his arrest. *Paul Fraughton, Salt Lake City Tribune.*

January 14, 1994. Jeff and Joyce Underwood in the Bannock County court room as James Wood is sentenced to death by lethal injection. The Underwoods wept as the judge read an account of their daughter's murder before pronouncing the sentence. At left is Jacque Christiansen, Bannock County Victim Witness Coordinator. *Doug Lindley, Idaho State Journal.*

June 1994. The community honors the memory of Jeralee Underwood with the release of pink balloons at her grave site. The Underwood family is in the foreground. The commemoration is an annual event in Pocatello. *Doug Lindley, Idaho State Journal.*

came out of the horseshoe-shaped drive without having seen Ford's car, Shaw drove back to the registration center and asked the clerk if anyone named Tommy Ford had registered at the camp-ground.

The clerk said Ford had stayed at the camp-ground for several weeks but had checked out on June 27. Shaw gave the clerk his business card and asked him to call if Ford returned. Although Shaw doubted Ford was the man they were looking for, his name would remain on the suspect list until the following Sunday.

When Shaw returned to the police station, he found new problems. The Latter-day Saints and other civic groups had been pressuring the police depart-ment for permission to conduct more volunteer foot searches. The searches were to cover rural areas along the highways and foothills south of town. Shaw's initial reaction had been to simply refuse permission for the searches. But the department was already under intense public pressure to find Jeralee and the man who had abducted her. To deny thou-sands of people the opportunity to help, especially when many of the searches were organized by the Latter-day Saints, could trigger a public relations nightmare.

Already the story of the daylight abduction of an outgoing, pretty, eleven-year-old girl from a deeply religious family had impacted the community as nothing before. Children, under the watchful eyes of adults, went door to door to almost every home in Pocatello, passing out posters with Jeralee's photo

and descriptions of her and the man who had kidnapped her. Pink ribbons began to appear, fluttering
in the summer wind from street signs, utility poles,
and car antennas.

Shaw's plan to deal with the public search teams
was simple. He had initially asked that the groups be
given permission to search areas that were well away
from places he believed the crime scene might actually exist. But the initial search areas would soon be
covered. Already, church and civic groups were asking for permission to search further south along the
Portneuf River and toward Black Rock Canyon. Both
areas could be reached by driving south on Authur
Street—the direction the abductor's car was seen
traveling—and by turning onto Portneuf Road, which
in turn offered access to Interstate 15. Shaw believed
those areas were logical "dumping grounds" if the
man had murdered the little girl shortly after her
abduction. Shaw desperately wanted both areas
searched by trained officers, but there simply was
not enough manpower available to search such a
large area.

Shaw flipped through his Rolodex and found the
phone number of Bob Green, a security supervisor
for the Department of Energy (DOE) at the Idaho
National Engineering Lab near Arco, some sixty
miles northwest of Pocatello. Beginning in World
War II and continuing through the cold war, INEL
was the center of some of the nation's most sensitive
research programs involving nuclear energy and pro-
pulsion. Security divisions at the lab were structured
to protect the perimeters and buildings of the huge

complex set in the remote Arco Desert. As such, they were equipped with sophisticated security technology that was the envy of law enforcement agencies throughout the region. Their arsenal included helicopters with infrared sensors able to detect intruders on the ground at night. The equipment is so sensitive that it can detect a rabbit from the infrared signature created by the animal's body heat.

Shaw had worked with Green on other searches. Now Shaw quickly got to the point: Could one of the DOE's infrared-equipped helicopters search along the Portneuf River and the foothills south of Pocatello? If Jeralee had been killed and her body dumped somewhere among the rugged canyons and hillsides south of the city, there was a good chance the infrared sensors would locate her before any evidence was destroyed by searchers plodding through the rugged terrain on foot. Green had followed the story of Jeralee's disappearance and readily agreed to make a helicopter and pilot available. Two officers from the Pocatello Police Department were to meet the helicopter at the Pocatello Airport at 10:30 that morning. To Shaw's surprise, Green never mentioned reimbursement for the use of the helicopter and pilot.

Thursday, July 1, 1993. The gray Bell 412HP helicopter, a newer, more powerful version of the U.S. Army's Huey, swept low over the mountains southeast of the city the sound of its rotors reverberating across the valley. As it turned east to follow Black

Rock Canyon, the infrared sensors picked up a heat source near the banks of the small creek along the canyon floor. Pilot Barry Nielson circled back and hovered above the source to pinpoint its location, then brought the helicopter down in a small clearing near the creek. The wash from the rotor kicked up a cloud of brown dust and debris.

Nielson and the two officers got out. Crouching low until they were clear of the blades, they made their way toward what appeared to be a mound of freshly-turned earth along the bank of the small creek. Carefully digging into the loose soil with shovels they had brought, they scooped away several inches of the dark-gray earth. Then a shape began to reveal itself in the shallow pit. They had unearthed the body of a large dog. It showed almost no sign of decay, for it apparently had been buried within the past day or two. After covering the make-shift grave, the three man went back to the helicopter. It lifted up and away from the small creek, and they resumed the search. Other than coyotes, deer, and other animals that scrambled away from the noise, no other heat sources were detected.

Later that day, Jeff and Joyce Underwood agreed to several television interviews in their home. Following Shaw's request that they attempt to personalize Jeralee, Joyce displayed some of Jeralee's clothing, including a hat and T-shirt identical to the ones she was wearing the day she left on her paper route. "Joyce and Jeff Underwood are searching for anything that might help them find their daughter," said the reporter, as the camera shifted to a close-up of a framed photo of Jeralee in the Underwoods' living room. "Photos of eleven year-old Jeralee, even her dishwashing duty list, hang as reminders that she never left home." The camera then cut to Jeff and Joyce standing next to each other in their kitchen. Speaking to the camera, Jeff said he was "trying to do a...few things around the home to keep my mind off what's happened...and kinda relieve...relieve some of the pain." The reporter continued, "Jeralee is one of six Underwood children, an outstanding student, vice president of her student council, who showed off her clogging skills during a recent school talent contest." Video clips then showed Jeralee as she clogged on the stage of her school auditorium.

The news segment ended with comments from Jeralee's younger sister Jennifer. The six-year-old, with thick auburn hair like Jeralee's and a few freckles sprinkled across the bridge of her nose, said almost inaudibly, "I'm scared." Her eyes lowered, and she was silent for a moment. Then Jennifer continued, "I want Jeralee to come back...I'm praying that she will come back."

Across town, Dave Haggard packed a few more supplies for a Fourth of July camping trip in his camper. He noticed that James Wood's Buick was gone. Haggard knew Wood was inside the house. When he had seen the car last night, it was parked on the other side of his camper.

Curious, Haggard walked toward the pasture in back, where he kept the old cars and trucks he was trying to sell. Wood's Buick was parked in the dry brown grass on the other side of an old white Cadillac limousine. Wood must have moved the car sometime last night. Haggard had suspected his cousin was trying to hide the car when Wood parked it behind the camper. Now he was sure of it.

Later in the day, Haggard and Wood drove into Pocatello and went to several garage sales but did not find anything interesting. On the way back to Chubbuck, Wood was unusually quiet and subdued.

Haggard did not give Wood's mood a lot of thought. He locked the house. They got in the camper and headed north, toward Idaho Falls. They were on their way to McCoy Creek, a beautiful, remote camping area near the western slope of the Tetons. Several other members of Haggard's family were to join them for a Fourth of July camp-out and family reunion.

19

Detective Shaw was still at his desk at midnight Friday when Donna Monroe, the chief's secretary, came into his office and handed him yet another stack of tip sheets. Like many others, Donna had volunteered to work late.

Shaw took the stack of tip sheets and leaned back in his chair to read them. Like the hundreds of others that Shaw had read, most of the sheets named someone the caller believed might be involved in Jeralee's disappearance. Several were from women who were sure their ex-husbands or boyfriends were capable of abducting a young girl.

But one tip came from a woman who had identified herself as Jane Pierce. "You should check out a nephew of mine," in connection with the kidnapping of Jeralee, she had said. "His name is James E. Wood."

When the operator who took the call asked Pierce why she believed her nephew might be involved, she had replied, "He spent time in prison for cutting up two girls." The caller also said her nephew had only lived in Pocatello for a short time and was staying with a relative named Dave Haggard. She gave the address and phone number of Haggard's house in Chubbuck. The caller described her nephew as being "strange." Asked for a physical description, she said Wood was 5'9" tall, had short brown hair, and weighed about 180 pounds. The caller also told the officer that her nephew owned a 1984 brown-and-tan Buick Century with the Idaho license plate number 1B47579. Before hanging up, the caller said Wood and Haggard had left earlier in the day for a Fourth of July camping trip. But she did not know where they were camping.

Shaw read through the rest of the tip sheets and put them with the others that required no immediate action. He took the sheet naming James E. Wood and walked outside. "Run a computer check on a Mr. James E. Wood," Shaw told one of the stenographers.

The computer check turned up three people named James E. Wood in the area with criminal histories. But none of their criminal records matched the profile. Still, the caller's description of Wood as "strange" and the fact that he was living with a relative matched Shaw's profile of the person likely to have abducted Jeralee.

The next morning, Shaw had Detective Linn drive to Chubbuck with a Polaroid camera to see if the

Buick Century the caller had described was there. Linn drove past Haggard's house, then parked on the shoulder and walked out into the pasture. Among the eight or nine old cars and trucks parked in the pasture, he saw the Buick, hidden from the road by the weathered Cadillac limousine. He took two shots of the car, one from the rear showing the license plate.

When Detective Linn returned with the Polaroids of Wood's Buick, Shaw had him take one to Ron Phipps, who had seen the car speed across Main Street the day Jeralee was abducted. Shaw took the other photo and drove to Blanche Tucker's house.

Although it was early on a Saturday morning, Blanche came to the door looking as if she had just returned from the beauty parlor. As Shaw walked inside, he was struck by how much the living room reminded him of his grandmother's house, always neat and tidy, as if she expected company to walk in at any minute. The furniture looked clean and polished, as if Blanche went to great pains to take care of it. As Shaw followed Blanche into her living room, he saw her mother sitting in a chair near the window. Her mother was in her nineties, with thinning white hair, dressed in a bathrobe and slippers. She smiled weakly and nodded toward Shaw.

"Sit down, Mr. Shaw," Blanche said, motioning toward the sofa. She sat down on the sofa near Shaw as he opened a manila envelope and took out the Polaroid of Wood's Buick.

"Mrs. Tucker, is this the car you saw the little girl pushed into?" he asked, handing her the photographs.

She took the photo and studied it carefully.

"Well, I can't say for sure it is," she said thought-fully.

Shaw said nothing as Blanche studied the photos.

"But it does look like the one I saw. And I believe the color's the same."

"So you can't say for sure, but you believe this could be the car?"

"Oh, yes, it could be," she replied.

Shaw was satisfied. He put the photos back in the envelope and stood up to leave. "Well, thank you, Mrs. Tucker," he said.

"Mr. Shaw," Blanche said, "I believe I know where Jeralee is."

Puzzled, Shaw sat down again. Blanche explained that she and some of her "psychic friends" had followed Jeralee's psychic trail to Lava Hot Springs, a small tourist town in the mountains about thirty miles outside Pocatello.

"Mr. Shaw," Blanche said, "I know she's somewhere near Lava Hot Springs. Can you take me down there?"

Shaw tried to explain that he was too busy, but Blanche was insistent. Blanche was absolutely sure she could pick up the little girl's psychic trail again if only someone would drive her to Lava Hot Springs. Shaw found himself in a dilemma. Blanche was one of only two eyewitness in the case, and the only one who actually saw Jeralee being pushed into the car. He knew that if anything came of the lead on James E. Wood, he would need Blanche's cooperation.

"I'll see what I can do," Shaw said reluctantly as he got up to leave. Later that day, he phoned Major Lorin Nielson, the undersheriff of Bannock County. Nielson listened as Shaw explained the situation with Blanche.

"I know it's a wild goose chase," Shaw said, "But it would help us out if you could have somebody drive her down there."

Nielson agreed to go himself. When he returned to Pocatello a few hours later, he called Shaw at his office.

"Well, I ended up with just what I thought I would," Nielson said.

"What's that?" Shaw asked.

"An empty tank of gas."

When Detective Linn returned to the station after showing the photos of Wood's Buick to Ron Phipps, the other witness who had seen the abductor's car, he went to Shaw's office.

"Phipps couldn't give us a positive ID," Linn said, placing the Polaroid of Wood's Buick on Shaw's desk. "But he did say the color was the same. He was sure of that."

But Wood was out of town, camping at some unknown location. All they could do was wait until he came back. Even then, there was little Shaw could do other than put Wood under surveillance. The man could not be arrested simply because a relative had named him as a suspect and because he had a criminal record. But based on what little information they had on Wood, he did seem to match the profile. Wood was added to a short list of suspects.

It was almost three o'clock in the morning when Shaw left the station and went home. As he drove down a deserted Fourth Street, he saw a pink ribbon tied to a utility pole. Within moments he drove past the subdivision where the Underwoods lived. He saw the back of the Underwoods' house. The lights in their kitchen were still on.

On that Friday afternoon when Dave Haggard and James Wood left for McCoy Creek, Haggard pulled his camper in at a busy convenience store near the small town of Palisades, Idaho. The parking lot was filled with cars and four-wheel drives, some towing boats on trailers, others with rubber rafts on top. As the two walked toward the convenience store, Wood hesitated for a moment, then opened the glass door and went inside. Taped to the door was a "Missing" poster bearing the image of Jeralee Underwood.

"Have they found that little girl yet?" Haggard asked the young clerk behind the counter. "No," said the girl, "but I hear they're bringing in a psychic to help find her."

Later that afternoon, after Haggard and Wood had set up camp at McCoy Creek, other members of Haggard's extended family began to arrive at the campsite. By late evening, as the sun was setting, charcoal grills glowed as the adults prepared the evening meal. As family members sipped cold beers and chatted, Wood sat in a folding lawn chair. He was quiet and seemed distracted.

When the conversation around the campfire turned to the little girl who was missing, Wood sat upon the edge of his chair. He said nothing. He appeared not to be listening. After a few minutes, he excused himself and went inside Haggard's camper. They all wondered why Wood had gotten up and gone to the camper. Because they were talking about the little girl? Usually, everyone agreed, he would be enjoying the conversation. Instead, "Jimmy" had kept to himself most of the day.

"Did you notice how when everybody was talking about the little paper girl that's missing, Jim never said a word?" one family member asked.

"He acted like he'd never heard about it," replied another.

"I'll bet he didn't spend ten minutes outside that camper all afternoon," someone else remarked.

Another reminded the group of the letters Wood's half brother Ernest Arnold had written to several relatives in Idaho when he found out that Wood had moved to Pocatello. In the letters, Ernest had warned them about "Jimmy."

What about the teenage girl who was raped last fall, the one whose little sister was in the car when it happened? The police drawing in the newspaper looked a lot like "Jimmy." Remember how Jim shaved off his goatee and stopped wearing his blue-jean jacket, the one with the fleece lining, after the paper said the man who raped the girl had been wearing one just like it?

At last, someone around the campfire voiced what they had all been thinking: "I think he had something to do with kidnapping that little girl."

"He stayed out all night the day that little girl was

taken," Haggard recalled. "I saw him when he came in early the next morning. He looked like he had been up all night, but the first thing he did was to vacuum out his car. Then he hid it behind my camper."

It rained most of the next morning. Later, when the rain stopped, Wood opened the door to the camper and looked out. Haggard and two or three other family members were sitting in the folding lounge chairs. Wood stepped down from the camper and started toward them.

"You know," Haggard said aloud as Wood approached, "whoever kidnapped that little girl ought to be taken downtown and hung up on a wall and shot."

Wood said nothing, Haggard noticed. Wood's silence only heightened their suspicion.

Later Saturday morning, Detective Scott Shaw and the other officers checked out tips as they came in. Detective Brennan drove out to Dave Haggard's house, but apparently no one had returned from the camping trip.

Just before noon, Shaw decided to try the KOA campground again in case Tommy Ford had returned. Shaw doubted Ford was connected with Jeralee's disappearance, but the fact that four different callers had named him as a suspect compelled Shaw to check Ford out.

Driving out Pocatello Creek Road, Shaw turned into the campground. As he rounded a curve on the dirt road leading to the campsites, Shaw noticed a car matching the description of Ford's car he had gotten from the DMV. The car was parked next to a small tent. Shaw pulled in behind the car and opened his notebook to check the tag number. It *was* Ford's car. Shaw pulled up beside the tent. Just as he opened the car door, he heard someone un-zipping the tent flap.

"Are you Tommy Ford?" Shaw yelled.

Ford stopped halfway out of the tent with a surprised look on his face.

"I'm with the police," Shaw said loudly. "Crawl on out of there; I need to talk to you!" As Ford crawled out of the tent, Shaw held out his badge.

"You got ID?" Shaw asked.

Ford reached in his back pocket and got out his wallet. To Shaw, Ford looked genuinely puzzled. For a split second, Shaw felt a small twinge of pity for Ford.

"I've been looking for you for three days," Shaw said, glancing at Ford's driver's license. "Where have you been?"

"I've been in Yucca City, in California," Ford said.

"For what?"

"To visit my mom and dad."

Shaw took a small notebook from his pocket. "Give me their names and a phone number," he said.

Ford complied. Answering Shaw's rapid-fire questions, Ford said he had left Pocatello on Sunday, June 24, and had arrived in Yucca City on Monday, the day before Jeralee was abducted. Then he had stayed three days at his parent's home and had arrived back in Pocatello last night. Shaw had him recite the route he had taken to Yucca City, taking notes as Ford talked.

It was only then that Ford asked what was going on, why he was being questioned.

"I'm concerned about something that happened in town while you were gone," Shaw said. He was beginning to sense that Ford had nothing to hide.

"Do you mind if I search your belongings?" Shaw asked. Ford shrugged his shoulders. "Sure, go ahead," he said. He gave Shaw permission to search everything, including his car. Shaw found nothing, other than the fact that Ford was remarkably well organized. Inside the small tent, his clothes were neatly folded and arranged in his suitcases. Even his underwear and towels, which he had stored in black plastic garbage bags, were sorted and nearly folded.

"What are you doing living in a tent, anyway?" Shaw asked when he finished looking through Ford's car.

Ford dropped his gaze. "My wife and I separated a few weeks back, and I didn't have anywhere else to live," he said. He explained that he didn't have a job but wanted to stay in Pocatello so that he could try to work things out with his wife. "I'm just staying out here to save money," he said. "It's too expensive to stay in a motel room or rent an apartment."

Ford seemed genuine. But there was still the remark Ford had allegedly made about "little girls."

"You spend some time at the Friendship Club, don't you?"

"I go there sometimes," Ford said, looking at Shaw. "Why, did something happen there?"

"You ever make a comment in the Friendship Club about having sex with little girls, something about 'breaking 'em in right?' "

Ford seemed taken aback by the question. "No, sir," he said emphatically. "No, I've never said anything like that!"

Shaw believed him. Thinking about the four regulars who had called the tip line, he asked Ford, "Why do you hang around that place?"

Again, Ford shrugged his shoulders. "I don't know," he said. "Just to be around people, I guess."

When you're there, do you talk to people a lot, sit by yourself, what?"

"I keep to myself, mostly," Ford said.

Shaw looked at Ford. The computer check had discounted a caller's comment about Ford having served time in prison. The fact that Ford kept to himself in the bar must have automatically made some of the regulars think he was weird. As far as Shaw could tell, he seemed like a decent type. Just lonely.

"You planning to be here for a while?" Shaw asked, as he opened the door of his car to go back to the police station.

"Yes, sir," Ford answered.

"OK, thanks," Shaw said.

When Shaw got to his office, he phoned Ford's parents in California. They confirmed that their son had driven down for a visit. He had arrived on Monday and had left to go back to Idaho on Friday.

Shaw thanked them and hung up. Then he opened a road atlas and checked the route Ford said he had taken to and from Yucca City. The mileage was about right for the time Ford said he had been on the road.

After he verified Ford's story, Shaw put away the atlas and glanced out the open door of his office. Even though it was Saturday, almost everyone in the department was working.

Shaw thumbed through the "promising" stack of tip sheets. He took out the four sheets that had named Tommy Ford as a suspect and put them with the hundreds of other sheets that did not warrant action. At the top of the thin stack of tip sheets that were promising was the one naming James E. Wood as a suspect.

Near McCoy Creek on Sunday morning, July 4, Dave Haggard began loading gear into the camper for the trip back to Pocatello. The trip had not been much fun for anyone, and not just because it had rained most of the time. The idea that "Jimmy" might be involved with the abduction of the little girl cast a pall over everyone's mood. In silence, Wood helped Haggard get ready to leave, packing food into coolers, stowing the *chaise longues*. Occasionally Haggard tried making a light comment, but Wood did not respond. Wood did not seem like himself.

"He was just out of character," whispered Haggard to one of the relatives later. "Like he was down, maybe a little nervous. He was just different."

After arriving back at Haggard's house that afternoon, Wood leaned back in one of the recliners in front of the big-screen TV. Outside, a young cousin who had become friends with Wood parked his car and ran into the house. The cousin's girlfriend came in, too, along with another young couple.

"Hey, Jimmy," the cousin shouted when the teenagers marched into the den and saw Wood seated in the recliner. "We're goin' up to Idaho Falls to watch the fireworks at the river tonight. Come on and ride up with us!"

A Fourth-of-July fireworks display was held each year just after dusk along the banks the Snake River near downtown Idaho Falls. One of the best places to view the fireworks was from the western bank of the Snake, near the railroad trestle north of downtown. There, a shallow diversion dam pooled the swiftly moving water just before it cascaded over the top of the dam in a smooth, white sheet. From the western bank, it was possible to see the fireworks as they exploded into brilliant colors high in the night sky and at the same time see their reflection in the dark waters behind the dam.

Wood seemed tired, his face drawn and pale. "No," he said quietly, "I believe I'll pass." He reached back for his wallet and took out two twenty-dollar bills.

"Here," he said, holding the money toward the teenagers. "Take this and buy yourselves a treat."

"Don't you want to go?" the boy asked, taking the money.

"Not this time," Wood said. "Y'all run on and enjoy yourselves."

20

Just before eight o'clock on Monday morning, a second tip sheet naming James Wood as a suspect in the Underwood case reached Scott Shaw's desk. The call was taken by Chief James Benham's secretary. The caller only identified herself as "a cousin of James Wood," adding that Wood might also be using the alias "James Johnson." When the secretary asked the caller why she believed Wood might be involved in Jeralee Underwood's disappearance, the caller said she remembered a case last fall when a young girl was abducted and raped while warming up her car. At the time, the caller said, she thought the description of the rapist in the newspaper fit her cousin James Wood. The caller also said Wood had friends who lived in the neighborhood where Jeralee delivered papers.

Dave Haggard left his house early on Monday morning. He was scheduled to begin a job he had contracted for, but first he had to pick up the linoleum he had ordered for the job. But when he got to the building supply company just after they opened, he was told the shipment had not arrived. Haggard called and rescheduled the job, then drove back home. As he turned into the driveway, he noticed the Ford Ranger pickup he had bought from Wood was gone. Wood's Buick was still there, parked behind the old Cadillac limousine.

Haggard went inside and got the keys to the Cadillac, then walked out to the pasture. It took a few tries before the old limousine started. When it finally turned over, he revved the engine for a moment or two, then put it in gear and pulled it forward one car length. Wood's Buick was no longer hidden from the road. *We'll see how he reacts to this*, Haggard said to himself.

Haggard went inside to the kitchen, poured himself a cup of coffee, and sat down by the window. He was sure Wood had taken the Ford Ranger, and he was irritated that Wood had not first asked permission. While he was waiting for Wood, Haggard phoned his sister. He told Pearl about the conversations he and some of the other family members had at McCoy Creek. They all thought Wood might have been involved in the newspaper girl's disappearance.

Pearl told Haggard that she had arrived at the same conclusion over the weekend, especially after talking with Liz Smith. Liz told Pearl that Wood was at her house the day Jeralee came to collect, and that

Wood left just after the little girl departed. Liz said Wood told them he was going to the store for a six-pack and would be right back. He never returned.

Haggard was still sitting at the kitchen table almost two hours later when he heard the pickup pull into the driveway. Within a minute or two, Haggard heard the sound of the shop vacuum coming from the garage. Haggard had intended to confront Wood about borrowing the truck without permission. But when he heard the vacuum, he decided against it. Instead, he sat in the kitchen nursing his cup of coffee until Wood came in through the back door and went downstairs to his bedroom.

When he heard Wood's footsteps going down the back stairs, Haggard quietly got up and went outside. As he had expected, Wood had gone to the pasture and moved his Buick forward by a car length. Once again it was parked beside the old Cadillac limousine, out of sight.

Haggard went to the garage and opened the top of the shop vacuum. He lifted out the dusty dirt bag and locked it in a wooden cabinet near the workbench. Again he called his sister. "I'm going down to the police and tell 'em," he said.

By that time, another call had come into the police tip line. The caller gave her name as Betty Grimes, and said she wanted to talk to an officer about the Underwood case.

In his office, Shaw picked up his phone. "Shaw here," he said.

"Mr. Shaw, My name is Betty Grimes," the caller

began. "And I think that a cousin of mine might've got that little girl."

"Before we start, I need to get a number where I can reach you," Shaw said. He wrote her home number down. Shaw asked if there was a work number where she could be reached. Grimes told him she worked as a receptionist at a doctor's office and gave him the number. "But I can't be talking to anybody while I'm working," Betty insisted.

"OK," Shaw said after taking her office number, "Now, what's your cousin's name?" Shaw asked.

"It's James Wood, but everybody calls him 'Jim,' or 'Jimmy.' But his real name is James Wood."

"What makes you think he had something to do with the little girl?"

"Well, for one thing, he's got a friend who lives in the neighborhood where the little girl had a paper route, and he spends a lot of time over there," she said. The friend's name was "Lizzie" Smith.

Did anything else make Betty suspicious?

"Jimmy's cousin said he stayed out all night the night the little girl was missing. And when he did come home the next morning, his uncle saw him cleaning out his car."

"Who is the cousin?" Shaw asked.

"Look, I'm sorry, but I can't talk about this at my job," she said, and the line went dead.

Shaw took the tip sheet from Betty Grimes and went across to Detective Mike Brennan's office. Brennan was an Eastern transplant with thick, dark hair and a mustache. Even though he had been with the Pocatello Police Department for twelve years, he had never lost his Philadelphian accent.

Shaw handed Brennan the tip sheet. "She works at a doctor's office somewhere in town," he said. "Call and find out where it is, then go have a talk with her. She told me this James Wood has friends who live on Jeralee's paper route, then said she couldn't talk about it anymore. To hell with that garbage. We need to find out what she knows, NOW!"

Brennan looked at the tip sheet. He immediately recognized the name. "Captain Wilhelm just got a call from a Doctor Wheeler," Brennan said. "He told Wilhelm his receptionist had some information on the Underwood case. His receptionist is Betty Grimes."

"Get over to wherever she works and get a statement from her," Shaw replied.

When Brennan showed up at her office, Betty told him everything she knew about James Wood. Within an hour, Brennan was back at the police station in Shaw's office outlining what he had learned. Even though Wood was her cousin, Betty had never known Wood until he moved to Pocatello about six months ago. Grimes thought Wood had moved from Tyler, Texas, although she wasn't sure. Wood lived in Chubbuck with his cousin, Dave Haggard. Over the Fourth of July weekend, Betty had gone on a family camping trip to McCoy Creek. Wood had been there, along with Haggard and several other family members. Grimes said Wood acted "strange" during the camping trip. Whenever anyone mentioned Jeralee, Wood appeared uninterested in the conversation. He never had anything to say about the missing girl.

One evening, several family members had gotten together and discussed their suspicions about Wood. Several said they believed Wood was the person who had taken the little girl. During that conversation, Haggard told the others that Wood had stayed out all night the day Jeralee was abducted.

"When Wood showed up the next morning," Brennan said, "Haggard saw him wash the outside of his car and vacuum the inside."

"Did she know what kind of car he has?" Shaw asked.

"A 1984 brown-over-tan Buick Century," Brennan answered.

"I had Detective Linn get some photos of it over the weekend," Shaw said. "Does Grimes know if Wood's back from the camping trip?"

"He got back Sunday afternoon," Brennan said. "But listen to this. Apparently this guy Wood does spend lot of time near Main and Carter. Grimes said he's friends with a woman named Smith who lives in the neighborhood. She said Wood's over at her house all the time."

Shaw took a file folder from his desk and opened it. The folder held a list of the subscribers on Jeralee's route. Shaw ran his finger down the list and found an Elizabeth Smith on Main Street. Shaw continued down the list until he found Blanche Tucker's name. Her address was also listed as Main Street. Elizabeth Smith's house was next door to Blanche Tucker's.

Shaw felt the adrenaline racing through his veins. All along he had believed whoever took Jeralee either lived in the neighborhood or spent time with someone who did. Blanche had been adamant that Jeralee had not seemed nervous when she saw her talking to the man just before he shoved her into the car. Perhaps Jeralee knew the man, or at least had seen him before.

But Brennan was not finished. "This guy Wood's apparently been in prison before," he said. "Grimes thinks he did time for something involving young girls. And there's one other thing: Grimes believes he's the one that raped the girl back in the fall, the one where the guy grabbed the girl behind the Pizza Hut."

"She's the second one who thinks that," said Shaw, almost to himself. "I'll be damned."

"When did Grimes say Wood got back from the camping trip?"

"Yesterday," Brennan replied.

"Drive out to Haggard's house and see if the Buick's still there," Shaw said.

As Brennan left his office to go to Chubbuck, Shaw reached for the file folder containing the profile he had worked up on Jeralee's abductor. He read and reread the four-page profile, comparing it to the information Jane Pierce and Betty Grimes had provided about James Wood. Pierce had said Wood was "strange." He didn't have a steady job. He had been in prison. He had been in Pocatello only about six months. His car was almost ten years old. He spent time in the neighborhood where Jeralee was abducted.

Shaw thought back to his interview with Beth Edwards shortly after she was kidnapped and raped. Her abductor had repeatedly said, *I'm in control.* If it turned out to be the same man, this "control-freak" aspect of his personality also matched the profile. Other than his age, the profile fit Wood like a glove.

Within fifteen minutes of leaving Shaw's office, Detective Brennan phoned Shaw. Wood's Buick was still parked in the pasture beside Haggard's house. Brennan said he was on his way back to the station.

After Brennan's call, Shaw went upstairs to the front of the station, where a crew from the TV series *America's Most Wanted* had set up. The producers of the show had sent a crew to Pocatello to tape a segment on Jeralee's abduction and had requested an interview with Shaw. Although Shaw was sure Wood was the person they were looking for, perhaps the publicity from *America's Most Wanted* would prompt even more information on him. They would need more than what they had to get an arrest warrant.

While Shaw was being interviewed by *America's Most Wanted*, one of the stenographers called over the intercom. "There's a Mr. David Haggard out front," she said. "He wants to talk to somebody on the Underwood case."

Detective Brennan went to the lobby and introduced himself, then motioned Haggard to his office. Haggard seemed agitated and nervous. He began by telling Brennan essentially what Betty Grimes had said about Wood earlier that morning. After describing Wood's behavior during the family outing, Haggard told the detective that Wood had been sitting in the living room of Liz Smith's home when Jeralee stopped by to collect for the paper. Wood had seen the little girl when she came inside and left within moments of Jeralee's departure. "He said he was going to the store to get a six-pack of beer and come right back," Haggard said. "But he never did."

Brennan knew immediately that this was a key piece of information. While Betty Grimes and another caller had said that Wood spent time in the neighborhood near Main and Carter Streets, now Wood had been placed inside a house two doors down from where Jeralee was abducted. And he had left only minutes before the abduction.

"And I found out he packs a pistol, too," Haggard added.

"Does he keep it on him?" Brennan asked.

"Far as I know, he does."

"Have you seen it?"

"No, but I know he's got it. He showed it to one of the kids."

"Do you know what kind it is?"

"They say it's a little .22 automatic, a silver one."

Brennan wanted to know about Wood's Buick Century. He had seen it earlier that day. Was it still parked in the pasture?

"He ain't drove it since the morning he came home and cleaned it out," Haggard said, nervously tapping his fingers. "Except when he tried to hide it. He parked it between my camper and the boat the first time, and then he moved it between some of my cars in the pasture. Before that little girl was missing, he drove that car every single day. He hasn't drove it once since, except when he hid it in the pasture."

In fact, Wood had borrowed his truck without permission that very morning "because he was afraid to drive his Buick," Haggard said. "And he vacuumed the truck out, too, when he brought it back. When I saw him do it, I went out and got the bag out of the shop-vac and locked it up. It's the same bag that was in it when he cleaned out his Buick after he stayed out all night, too."

"Are you willing to turn the bag over to us?" Brennan asked.

"I will once you arrest him," Haggard said. "I already told you he packs a gun. What do you think he's gonna do if he finds out I've been talking to you or if he finds out I gave the vacuum bag to you? I know some of the family's already called on him," Haggard went on. "Why don't you just go out there and get him?"

Brennan explained that Wood couldn't be arrested just because someone suspected him of a crime, even when *several* people suspected him. But he assured Haggard that Wood was being watched.

"Hell," said Haggard. "If you're watching him, why didn't you get him when he left this morning?"

After taking Haggard's information, Brennan led Haggard to Shaw's office, where he repeated most of what he had just told Brennan. Shaw was especially interested in learning that Wood had been at Liz Smith's house when Jeralee came to collect. Shaw asked Haggard if he remembered what Wood was wearing the morning he came in after being out all night. Haggard told him Wood was wearing a black baseball cap and a dark plaid shirt. He also said Wood had "shaved his mustache off from the last time I had seen him."

"Does Wood have a steady job?" Shaw asked.

"No, he don't work a job," Haggard said. "He makes a little cigarette money from some paintings he sells now and then, but he hasn't had a regular job since he's been here." He added that it was known "in the family" that Wood had a prison record.

"Why was he in prison?" Shaw asked.

"He told me it was for passing checks," Haggard said. "But some of the family say it was for rape and cuttin' up a couple of girls."

Just before Haggard left, Shaw asked him if it was OK for the police to search his home. Haggard agreed.

"Would you be willing to sign a statement verifying what you told Detective Brennan and myself concerning James Wood?" Shaw asked.

"I'll sign a statement," Haggard said.

As Haggard left, Shaw turned to Brennan. "Go over to this Liz Smith's house and verify Wood was there when Jeralee came to collect. Call me with anything you get. I'll be at the prosecutor's office."

21

Bannock County Prosecutor Mark Hiedeman had been watching the late broadcast of the local news on television on June 29 when he saw the report that an eleven-year-old paper girl was missing. The early reports did not reveal that a witness had seen Jeralee being forced into a car. Hiedeman had assumed the young girl was probably a runaway and would soon return home. But as the days passed following Jeralee's disappearance, Hiedeman, like others in the law enforcement community, feared the worst.

Hiedeman had been in daily contact with investigators and knew there were suspects in the Underwood case. Still, Hiedeman was taken by surprise when Shaw rushed into his office at the Bannock County Courthouse and asked him to prepare an affidavit for a search warrant in the case.

Shaw sat down across from Hiedeman and reviewed the information they had on James Wood:
the call from Jane Pierce, Brennan's interview with
Betty Grimes, Dave Haggard's visit to the station, the
fact that Wood fit the profile of the man they were
looking for. While Shaw and Hiedeman organized
the information to be typed on the affidavit, Shaw
took a phone call from Detective Brennan. He was
at Liz Smith's house and had a statement from her
daughter, Tammy Retzloff. Tammy confirmed that
Wood had been at her house when Jeralee came in,
that he had left within minutes after Jeralee did, and
that he did not return for dinner. Liz Smith was at
work, Brennan said. He was on his way to the
collection agency where she worked and would call
again from there.

Shaw dropped the phone in its cradle and turned
to Hiedeman. "Mark," he said, "we're pushing this
thing this far, let's go for an arrest warrant."

Hiedeman looked up at Shaw. It was one thing
to go before a magistrate to present a probable cause
for a search warrant. But proving to a judge that you
had probable cause for an arrest warrant was another matter entirely, especially in this case. Jeralee
was under twelve years old. In Idaho, that meant the
charge would be first-degree kidnapping, a capital
offense.

Shaw knew what Hiedeman was thinking. "Mark,
this guy Wood's a con," Shaw said. "He's been in
prison. He knows the drill. He knows exactly what
to say. He'll smell it in a minute if he thinks we're
on a fishing expedition. What if he just says, 'Kiss my

ass, talk to my attorney'? Hell, he might even enjoy watching us running around all over the place."

Hiedeman paused. Based on what Shaw had told him, he felt Shaw had established probable cause for a search warrant. Haggard, the owner of the house were Wood lived, had indicated he would allow his property to be searched. But an arrest warrant for a capital offense?

"You say Haggard hid the dust bag from the vacuum Wood used to clean out his car?" Hiedeman asked Shaw.

"He did," Shaw said. "But he doesn't want to turn it over unless Wood's arrested. He's a little afraid of Wood, and I don't blame him."

"I think we've got enough to charge him," Hiedeman said. "Now all we have to do is convince Judge Box."

By the time both affidavits were printed out, Brennan had called from the office where Liz Smith worked. The statement she made matched that of Tammy Retzloff, her daughter. Both statements were included in the affidavits.

Just before five on Tuesday afternoon, Detective Shaw and Prosecutor Mark Hiedeman walked downstairs to the first floor office of Judge Gaylen Box. In his leather portfolio, Shaw carried the two affidavits of probable cause, one for a search warrant for Haggard's residence at Thyee Road and the Buick Century owned by Wood, the second for an arrest warrant for James Wood.

Judge Box listened as Shaw outlined his reasons justifying the warrants. In most cases, Judge Box approved—and sometimes disapproved—requests for warrants in his office. But this time was different.

"Let's go into court," Judge Box said, standing up.

As Judge Box went to his chambers, Shaw's heart sank. Did Judge Box want everything on record because he was going to deny the arrest warrant?

Shaw exchanged glances with Hiedeman as they went down the hall toward the courtroom. "Why is he going into court?" Shaw asked, looking at Hiedeman. "Are we screwed, or what?"

As they waited for Judge Box to enter the small courtroom from his chambers, Shaw and Hiedeman sat at the prosecutor's table. They were alone in the empty courtroom for a minute or two. Then Judge Box and a court clerk came in.

Shaw was placed under oath by the clerk. Then Hiedeman stood and began to question Shaw. Hiedeman asked a few questions about Shaw's background as an investigator, then shifted to what could "reasonably be expected to be found" in Haggard's house or in Wood's car.

When Hiedeman finished, Judge Box asked several short questions, confirming that Wood did in fact live in Haggard's house. When he concluded, Judge Box looked at Shaw and nodded. "Thank you, sir, you may step down."

Before Shaw could stand, Hiedeman rose from his chair. "If I may, Your Honor, one additional question comes to mind. I assume, Detective Shaw, that Mr. Haggard has no problem with your searching his residence. Is that correct?"

"No problem whatsoever," replied Shaw.

"He doesn't have a problem consenting to not only the search of his residence, but turning over the vacuum bag to the authorities?" asked Hiedeman.

"No, sir. The only problem Mr. Haggard has is that he is firmly convinced James Wood is the perpetrator of Jeralee's kidnapping, and he feels that he is in direct danger if he turns those items over to us."

"All right. Thank you," Hiedeman said. "That's all I have, Your Honor."

"You may step down," Judge Box said. Shaw stepped down and joined Hiedeman and Brennan at the counselor's table.

"From reviewing the affidavit of probable cause," said Judge Box, "and in considering the testimony that's been given at this hearing, the court does conclude that there is reason to believe that evidence of criminal activity may be located at said residence and may be located in or about the Buick Century bearing Idaho license number 1B47579."

After reciting his reasons for granting the search warrant into the record, Judge Box looked at Hiedeman. "Do you have anything further you want to add?"

"No, not yet, Your Honor," Hiedeman said cryptically.

"OK," said Judge Box. "Based upon what I've recited on the record and other factors not recited on the record...the court will issue the search warrant at this time. And if you have nothing further, Mr. Hiedeman, we'll conclude."

Hiedeman rose to his feet, interrupting the judge. "In light of what's happened here, Your Honor,"

Hiedeman said, "I have prepared a warrant and complaint charging James Wood with first-degree kidnapping."

Shaw's pulse raced as he saw Judge Box raise his eyebrows.

Hiedeman continued. "I think because the probable cause for the request for the complaint is contained primarily in the affidavit the court has already received, the affidavit not only shows probable cause to search that residence and the described vehicle, but I think...it also shows probable cause to believe that Mr. Wood has committed a kidnapping. I've prepared a warrant complaint to that effect, and I ask the court to consider issuing that at this time. Also..."

Now it was Judge Box's turn to interrupt. "We'll go off the record at this time," he said to the clerk. Then he left the bench and went into his chambers.

Still seated at the witness stand, Shaw feared the worst. He had decided to "go for broke" and push for an arrest warrant. Now Judge Box clearly appeared upset at their unexpected request for an arrest warrant. Shaw glanced anxiously at Brennan, as if seeking moral support, and then at his watch. It was almost six. He wondered what had happened when Haggard returned home from the police station. Shaw turned as he saw Judge Box returning from his chambers. To Shaw's relief, the judge had gone to his chambers to check an appointment time.

"Are you ready to proceed, Mr. Hiedeman?" Judge Box asked.

"Yes, Your Honor," Hiedeman replied.

"We're back on record," Judge Box said.

Hiedeman began by questioning Shaw about the door-to-door canvassing that had taken place. He asked Shaw to explain exactly what Blanche Tucker had seen on the day Jeralee was pushed into the car, beginning from the moment Jeralee arrived at her door to collect. After several questions, Hiedeman led Shaw to the point when Blanche saw Jeralee talking to the man beside his car.

"What did Blanche see then?" Hiedeman asked Shaw.

"She said she saw Jeralee talking to this man," Shaw said. "It seemed very casual. She didn't perceive any fear, any agitation, any apprehension. In fact, there was no sign whatsoever anything was wrong. The immediate impression was that Jeralee knew the person."

"What side of the car did he force her in?" Hiedeman asked.

"The driver's side, front seat."

Hiedeman asked Shaw if he had spoken to Jeralee's parents.

"Yes, sir. Several times a day since the occurrence."

"Did you talk to them at all about giving Jeralee specific warnings about talking to strangers?"

"Yes, I did," Shaw answered. "That was an area of conversation. Both parents told me they were very much aware of the hazards involved when a young girl is out on the streets by herself...they said not once, but several times, on a continuing basis, they talked to her about avoiding strangers, not getting into anyone's car."

Then Hiedeman shifted the focus to Liz Smith's house. "Is it right next door to the Tucker residence?"

"Yes, sir."

"So Jeralee would have been at the Smith residence just moments before she was at the Tucker residence?"

"That's correct," said Shaw. "And that is...a very significant point."

"Why is that?" Hiedeman asked.

"Because Mr. Wood only had to walk a few minutes, at the most, from the Smith residence, get in his car, and drive his car up to the corner of Carter and Main. If he was parked within half a block, or within a block...it would certainly take less than two or three minutes to get in his car and start it and drive over to Carter and Main. And that gives us the time for his vehicle to be moved while Jeralee is inside the Tucker home collecting. The time estimated on that is five minutes. Usually, it takes a few minutes just to write out a check and hand it to her."

"And that would certainly explain why she might appear to know this person?"

"Absolutely," said Shaw.

Hiedeman said he had no further questions for Shaw.

Still seated on the witness stand, Shaw could barely hear Judge Box as he spoke to the clerk. If he were denied an arrest warrant, it would be a disaster. True, Judge Box had already approved the search warrant. But what if Wood simply refused to talk? They had no physical evidence to link him with

Jeralee. And if they did not find any evidence at Haggard's house, then what?

"Detective Shaw," Judge Box asked, "is there anything more you wish to add, based upon your training or experience, that you think the record should reflect in your application here?"

"Yes, sir, there is," Shaw said.

He wanted the judge to understand that he believed Jeralee's abduction had been an act of compulsion committed by Wood. By contrast, an organized offender, Shaw explained, was someone who did not act from compulsion and therefore would not have taken Jeralee from such a high-risk location. Instead, he would have waited until she was in a more secluded area, such as the industrial area three blocks south. There, the chances were less that anyone would have witnessed the abduction.

"From the moment the report came in," Shaw continued, "I believed Jeralee's abductor was either someone who she collected from or who had been present when someone else paid her. At that moment, the person made a compulsive decision to abduct Jeralee. A compulsive act is an act of a disorganized offender. And James Wood has many, many traits that match the profile of a disorganized offender." As he spoke, Shaw grew nervous. Was he rambling? "We believe the event was sexually motivated," he continued. "In going along with the profile, we also have to conclude that Jeralee was murdered and disposed of within a fairly short time after her abduction." Shaw stopped and glanced pensively at Hiedeman and Brennan.

Judge Box looked down at his notes. "When you canvassed the neighborhood, did you turn up anything to indicate another suspect other than Wood was in the area at the time?"

"No, sir," answered Shaw. "We did not."

"Do you have anything further, Mr. Hiedeman?" the judge asked, glancing toward the prosecutor's table.

"Just a couple of things," Hiedeman said as he stood and approached Shaw. "Detective Shaw, specifically, what was it that Mr. Haggard told you about the history of Mr. Wood?"

"Mr. Wood correlates with our profile. He is a loner. He is very unstable. He's lived in the area about six months. He'll do a part-time job here or there just for cigarette money while mooching off a relative. His probable prison time Mr. Haggard verified."

"Did he (Haggard) tell you specific crimes?" Hiedeman asked.

"He specifically told me rape and said, 'he (Wood) did time for cutting up two little girls.' We're not able to verify that. Those crime reports are in the archives in Louisiana. We have no chance of getting the records for several days. People describe Wood as strange... less than a high school diploma, rather uneducated, low socioeconomic background. I could go on if you'd like."

"Have you checked to find out if Wood did in fact have a criminal record?" Heideman asked.

"Yes," said Shaw.

"And what does that show?"

"He does have a prior record for robbery, aggravated battery, and rape."

"But you don't know," Hiedeman continued, "whether this aggravated battery or the rape concerned 'cutting up two little girls' as Mr. Haggard had told you?"

"No, sir," Shaw said. "I have no information on that."

"All right," Hiedeman said. "I don't have anything else right now."

Shaw stepped down. His mind was racing. Had they been thorough enough?

Finally Judge Box issued his ruling. "I've reviewed the attachments to the affidavit of probable cause and conclude from all of this evidence that a warrant for the arrest of James Wood be issued." The bond was to be set at $750,000.

22

Elated, Detective Shaw drove back to the police station. The arrest warrant issued by Judge Box gave Shaw confidence that his decision to "go for broke" was correct, at least up to this point. But now came the real test. When James Wood was arrested, could he be persuaded to talk? Under Idaho law, Wood had the right to a preliminary hearing within ten days. If no evidence linking Wood to Jeralee was found by that time, and Wood refused to talk, he would have to be released.

Shaw rushed to his office and reviewed the profile he had developed. He wrote down his ideas on how to best orchestrate Wood's arrest.

When the offender is identified, the profile read, his arrest should be carried out in such a manner that leaves no doubt in [his] mind that he has been "caught." He has experience with the judicial system and will present a very negative attitude to being interviewed unless he is convinced he has been caught and there is no way out.

The offender will be very sensitive and is most likely to respond to respectful treatment and to the [belief] that the officer conducting the interview understands him and...has an understanding of why the offense occurred. The officer should not convey the impression that he has judged the offender. The use of hard interrogative words must be avoided; these include... "kidnapped," "kill," "body," or other words of a similar nature...

The interview will be excessive in the time required, so special attention to food, rest, and other necessities must be planned for.

The offender has probably perceived a great deal of his life as [him] being rejected. This could be used by the interviewing officer by providing unconditional acceptance and understanding. The offender will want to repay this kindness in the only way he is able...that is, by telling or providing a truthful account of the offense.

Outside Shaw's office, the news spread through the detective division that an arrest warrant for James Wood had been issued. Moreover, word had been received from Dave Haggard that Wood was at home, asleep in an easy chair in the front room. By then, Detective Brennan had returned from the courthouse. Mark Hiedeman and several of his deputy prosecutors had also arrived at the station. A briefing on the pending arrest was quickly organized, but almost no one had yet to be notified. It seemed as if everyone associated with the case had gathered outside the detectives' offices. Representatives from the Idaho State Police were also there, along with Bannock County Sheriff Bill Lynn and Undersheriff Lorin Nelson, the man who had driven Blanche Tucker to Lava Hot Springs.

It was decided that Chief Benham and Detective Brennan would make the arrest. Shaw would be close by but far enough away to be physically removed from the arrest. Once Benham and Brennan had Wood under control, Shaw would move in and take him from the two officers. Shaw would then isolate Wood from the officers who had made the arrest. Shaw's demeanor would be friendly and nonthreatening. His hope was to have Wood see him as an ally rather than a threat.

Shaw reminded everyone that he believed Wood had committed a capital offense. Wood also was reportedly armed. Chief Benham and Detective Brennan were to take physical control of Wood immediately, handcuff him, and check him for weapons. They were to treat Wood's arrest as they would the arrest of any other dangerous felon. Their weapons would be displayed and ready.

Shaw had another reason for wanting weapons displayed. Wood, he felt, was someone who desperately needed to feel in control. Having live firearms aimed at him would strip him of that control.

Shaw also wanted as many marked police cars as possible at Haggard's house within moments of the arrest. Arrangements were made with the Idaho State Patrol and the Chubbuck Police Department to make both marked and unmarked cars available to join units from the Pocatello Police Department and the Bannock County Sheriff's Department. With the exception of Chief Benham and Detective Brennan's car and the one driven by Shaw, the rest of the cars were to stay out of sight until Shaw had taken Wood to his car and closed the door. That would be the signal for the rest of the cars to converge on the scene and visually overpower Wood.

The sense of anticipation was mounting. Wood had served two terms in a state penitentiary. There was every possibility he would violently resist arrest. Shaw's decision to stage a choreographed arrest was intended to throw Wood off balance in the hope he might be persuaded to talk. But it was risky. A safer procedure would have been to simply surround Haggard's house with a SWAT team, telephone Wood, and order him to surrender.

At Dave Haggard's home, an American flag billowed from the flagpole on the side of the house. Wood's Buick sat between the limousine and another car.

Just before 7:30, Chief Benham and Detective Brennan pulled onto the grass in front of the house. Shaw, following behind, parked on the side of the road a few yards back from the driveway and stood a few paces behind them.

Inside, Haggard, nervously fingering a cigarette, watched from his kitchen window as the two unmarked cars pulled up.

Shaw and the two officers exchanged nods. Then Chief Benham and Detective Brennan walked up the concrete steps leading to the door. Brennan knocked, then stepped back. Shaw stood at the edge of the deck, as far from the door as possible. He reached down and drew his 10-millimeter Smith & Wesson semiautomatic from its holster and held it down to his side.

Inside, Wood snapped awake at the sound of Brennan's knock. He took a .357 magnum he had placed in the chair and cracked the door open. Wood looked cautiously at the men standing on the deck. Wood held his gun behind the door.

"Are you Mr. Wood?" asked Brennan. Neither Brennan nor Chief Benham had drawn their pistols.

"Yes?"

"Mr. Wood," said Brennan, "we'd like to talk to you for a minute."

Wood studied the two men for a moment, then glanced at Shaw. "Yeah," he said. "Just gimme a second." He closed the door and hastily stuffed the .357 down in the cushion of the big easy chair. Then he opened the door.

At that instant both Brennan and Chief Benham drew their pistols from holsters under the jackets.

"You're under arrest!" shouted Brennan as he

aimed his semiautomatic at Wood's face, grabbed him by the arm, and pulled him onto the deck.

"Face down!" Brennan shouted, "Face down!" Both policemen used their free hands to force Wood to the floor of the deck. While Benham held his pistol to Wood's head, Brennan straddled him and cuffed Wood's arms behind his back. Brennan patted Wood's waistband and ran his hands along the inseam of Wood's jeans. He had no weapons on him. Then the officers pulled Wood to his feet and pushed him toward the steps.

Shaw holstered his pistol and moved off the deck. As the two men led Wood down the steps, Shaw walked toward them. He took Wood by the arm. Brennan and Chief Benham dropped back.

"Geez," said Shaw, steering Wood toward his car. "They didn't have to do all that," feigning that the officers had used excessive force.

Wood looked at Shaw. "Well, Scott," he said. "How are you?"

Shaw was surprised Wood called him by name. "Sounds like you've been watching the news, Jim." Then he opened the passenger door and seated Wood inside.

Seconds later, two fast-moving caravans of cruisers, strobe lights flashing, raced toward Dave Haggard's house.

From inside Shaw's car, Wood watched as the lead cars wheeled into the driveway. Officers spilled out, among them the Pocatello Police Department's SWAT team, dressed in blue/black combat fatigues and armed with 9-millimeter MP-5 submachine guns, M-16 assault rifles, and shotguns.

Uniformed officers and sheriff's deputies went inside Haggard's house to search. The plainclothes officers, at Shaw's instructions, began to file by the passenger side of Shaw's car. As they did, they stopped and peered inside at Wood. At the briefing, Shaw had instructed the officers they were to give Wood the most contemptible look they could muster. Again, the intent was to intimidate.

As the first few officers paused to glare at Wood, he returned their stares. Then he turned away and lowered his eyes. He turned toward Shaw.

"What's this all about?" he asked.

Shaw was surprised by the almost childlike quality of Wood's voice. Yet Shaw said nothing. He took a large manila envelope from the seat between them. He pulled out a photo of Wood's car. The photograph had been taken from the rear of the Buick, the license plate clearly visible. In the white margin at the top of the photo was a handwritten date, June 29, the day Jeralee had disappeared. Shaw put the photo face up in Wood's lap.

"That's my car," said Wood.

"I know," said Shaw. "That's what happens when you screw up, Jim."

Shaw reached into the manila envelope again. This time, he carefully slid out an eight-by-ten color portrait of Jeralee. He placed it in Wood's lap. Wood's shoulders slumped and the color drained from his face.

Shaw left the photographs lying in Wood's lap as

he started the car. Shaw said nothing as they drove. Minutes later they passed the Pizza Hut where Beth Edwards had been abducted. They drove past the McDonald's where Wood had eaten breakfast that first day in Pocatello. Wood gazed ahead in silence.

Once Wood was driven away, Haggard walked across the road and stood looking back at the surreal scene on his lawn. Police cars filled his yard. The flash of strobe lights bounced off his house. Neighbors began to gather in their yards to watch. One of Haggard's neighbors, taking in the scene with disbelief, came over and stood beside him.

"What do you think of my car auction?" Haggard joked.

23

When they reached the police station, Detective Shaw turned into the alleyway behind the building and drove into the parking lot. At the metal rear door, Shaw punched a code into the keypad. The buzzer sounded. He held the door open for James Wood, then guided the suspect down a brightly lit, tiled hallway to the detective division.

Shaw took Wood to his office and closed the door. Shaw turned Wood so that he faced away from him and removed the handcuffs. "Have a seat, Jim," Shaw said, nodding toward the three metal chairs facing his desk.

Wood, rubbing his wrists, sat down in the middle chair. He looked up at Shaw. Under the bright fluorescent glow of the overhead lights, Shaw studied the face of James Wood. He was forty-six, and his tired face seemed that of a man who had lived a hard life. His baby-fine brown hair had begun to recede at the hairline. The flesh under his deeply set eyes was dark and puffy. His head seemed almost too large for his narrow shoulders, yet his neck was thick. Wood's bare arms, though not heavily muscled, showed strength.

Wood wore blue jeans and a blue-green pullover with a low neck that revealed the upper part of his chest, the skin much whiter than his tanned face and arms. Scars were visible just above the neckline of his pullover. While in jail awaiting trial in Louisiana, Wood had been badly burned when a cellmate doused him with a flammable liquid and set him afire while he slept. Apparently Wood had been the instigator of the episode, for he had reportedly refused to share cigarettes with his cellmate and had taken all the blankets. The cellmate had waited and finally taken his revenge.

Shaw took a seat at his desk and began to advise Wood of his rights under the *Miranda* ruling. Shaw read the first sentence, then stopped and looked at Wood. "Do you understand what I've just told you?"

"I know my rights," Wood said matter-of-factly.

Shaw began to read again. At the end of each sentence, Shaw asked Wood if he understood what he had just heard. Each time, Wood answered, "Yes."

"You don't have to go into them all," Wood said. "I've been in the pen. I probably know my rights better than you do."

Shaw continued to read, still pausing after each

sentence. When he had read the entire statement, he asked Wood if he completely understood his rights.

"I understand them completely," Wood said. "And I'll talk to you."

"Can you read and write?" Shaw asked, ignoring Wood's offer to talk.

"Yes," replied Wood quietly.

Shaw handed Wood the rights form and asked him to read aloud the waiver of rights statement at the bottom.

Wood read the statement aloud.

"Do you understand what *pressure* means?" asked Shaw.

"Yes."

"Do you understand what *coercion* means?"

"Yes."

"After hearing and understanding your rights, do you wish to waive them and talk to me?"

"Yes," said Wood.

Shaw gave him a pen and asked him to sign the waiver of rights and date it.

Wood signed his name, then looked up. "I know it's July," he said. "But I don't remember what day it is."

"It's the sixth," said Shaw.

After Wood signed and dated the statement, Shaw folded it and put it on his desk. "You want a Coke, Jim?" he asked.

"That'd be good, Scott," Wood said, smiling. "My throat's gettin' a little dry."

Shaw asked one of the stenographers to go to the break room and get two Cokes.

While they waited, Shaw went back inside and sat down in the chair next to Wood. He made small talk about McCoy Creek and fishing until the stenographer knocked on the door with the Cokes.

Shaw closed the door and handed one of the soft drinks to Wood. Then he opened the manila envelope he had brought in from the car and took out the eight-by-ten color portrait of Jeralee. Shaw put it on the desk in front of Wood.

"Jim," Shaw said, sitting down next to Wood in front of the desk, "You've got a big problem here, and we've got a lot of things to work through here tonight."

Wood took a drink from his Coke and looked at the photo. "Yeah, I took her with me," he said in a flat, matter-of-fact voice. "I got her in my car, and I drove her down, down toward Salt Lake." Then he looked at Shaw. "But I let her out. I'm surprised she hasn't turned up by now."

"You're saying you took her, but you let her out, alive?"

"That's what I'm saying," Wood said. "Let her out down there, down toward Salt Lake, out by some farmer's field."

"Where exactly was the field, Jim?" Shaw asked.

"I don't know if I can tell you exactly," Wood said, as he took another drink from the can and wiped his mouth with the back of his hand. "Somewhere down south, some town off Interstate 15. Scott, I was drinking so much, everything was a blur."

Shaw had Wood describe his route after he

turned left on Arthur Street. Wood said that he did not know the name of the street, but he described driving south, past a golf course. He then turned onto a road that ran by a creek. He stopped by "some willows near a creek." But there were joggers in the area, so he left. Then, Wood said, he "hung a right" onto Interstate 15 heading south. He stopped at the first exit that had stores and bought a twelve-pack of beer at a truck stop. Wood remembered the exit led to Highway 34 because "there's a Highway 34 in Louisiana." He went back on the interstate and drove a while, then stopped at another convenience store, gassed up, and bought another twelve-pack of beer.

"That would've been Downey," Shaw said, when Wood described the exit. "How did you keep the little girl in the car while you bought beer and got gas?" Shaw asked.

"I just told her to stay down. I had her lie down on the floor, under the dashboard there. Told her to stay down, and I'd take her home to her mamma."

"And she just stayed there, on the floorboard?"

"Yes, sir, she did," Wood said. "Stayed right there, just like I told her to."

Wood said he then turned left over the interstate and drove for about an hour. He said he stopped near a sign that read Bear River.

"That's near Preston," Shaw said. "About and hour and a half from here," Shaw said patiently. "Then what?"

"Well," Wood said, "I just looked over at that little girl, and I decided I was going to take her back. I swear to God, Scott, I just decided I was gonna take her back. So I turned around close to a bridge, and I remember the sign said Bear River, and just past that was a big farmer's field with a little road going in it. I let her out right close to the road. I said, 'Honey, when I drive away, you walk right up to that road and somebody'll find you and take you home to mamma.' Wood's demeanor was a facade of caring.

"What time was it when you let her out?"

"I don't know exactly," Wood said, shaking his head ruefully. "It was still daylight, I remember." Then he looked at Shaw. "Scott, I'll tell you, I'd been on a drinking binge for about a week...things were just a blur."

Shaw knew Wood had not returned to Dave Haggard's house until the following morning. "Jim, I don't think you're telling me the truth here," he said. "I don't think you let that little girl out down there. And I don't think she's alive."

"Scott, I'll swear on a stack of Bibles, I let that little girl out, and I came on back to Pocatello. The last I seen of her, she was standing out there by that field."

Shaw didn't buy it, but Wood was sticking to his story. Shaw tried another tactic. "Jim," he said softly, "I know an awful lot about you. I know you've had a rough life, a life nobody deserves, and I feel bad about that. Things just haven't always worked out the way you wanted them to, have they?"

"That's right," Wood said, taking the last sip of Coke from the can, his eyes cutting to meet Shaw's.

"That's the gospel truth." Wood took the empty can and crushed it flat with his hands and put it in the trash can beside Shaw's desk.

"Scott," he said, turning to look at Shaw, "Do you mind if I smoke?" He reached into the front pocket of his pullover and pulled out an almost empty pack of Marlboro cigarettes. There was a matchbook inside the cellophane of the pack. Nothing had been taken from Wood in the search on Haggard's deck.

Shaw hesitated. One of Chief Benham's hard-and-fast rules was that no one—no one—smoked inside the building. Even though there was a cigarette machine in the break room, there were no ashtrays anywhere in the station. Anyone who absolutely had to have a cigarette could stand outside to smoke. But Shaw also knew that he had to make Wood feel comfortable.

"Sure, Jim," Shaw said. "Let me find an ashtray."

Shaw got up and went outside. Benham and several other officers were standing outside, out of view of Shaw's window.

"He said he took her, but he's saying he let her out alive near Preston," Shaw said. "But I know the prick's lying, and now I've gotta to find him an ashtray." After looking in several offices and finding no ashtrays, Shaw went back to his office and closed the door.

"I guess the city's just too cheap to buy any ashtrays," Shaw laughed as he sat down next to Wood. He slid his half-empty Coke over in front of Wood. "This is the best I could do."

Wood tapped a cigarette out of the pack, brought

it to his mouth, and lit it. He shook the match out and laughed. "Boy," he said, dropping the match in the Coke can. "That *is* pretty cheap. Just about every place you go's got an ashtray someplace."

Shaw began to talk about Wood's past again. Shaw knew that statistically Wood, like most sexual offenders of his type, probably came from a broken home or dysfunctional family. Most, like Wood, were physically or emotionally abused as children.

"Look, Jim," Shaw said. "I know you haven't had any breaks in life, that everything you've tried to do in life's turned out wrong. And I know you had a rough childhood, that people have abused you."

"How do you know so much about me?" Wood asked earnestly. "I swear, it's like you can read my mind."

"I know you were abused by your parents," Shaw said.

"No, I wasn't!" Wood snapped. He had been abused, all right, but not by his real parents. His *real* parents had been good to him. The abuse came from his stepfather, a man from Lincoln, Idaho. His mother had married him after Wood's real father was sent to prison. Then, after his mother died, Wood said he was physically abused by his adopted parents. His real mother and father, Wood insisted, had been good to him.

"How did your mother die, Jim?" Shaw asked.

Wood grew emotional, his voice breaking. Wood said that when he was eight, his mother was working in a potato processing plant. One day the plant caught fire, Wood said, and he watched the blaze from his schoolroom across the street. He jumped out of the classroom window and ran toward the fire. There, he said, people held him back. He turned to a "woman in a gray wool dress" and put his arms around her, but the woman pushed him away. His mother died from burns suffered in the fire.

"I can still remember the smell of that woman's dress," Wood said. From that point on, I started to hate women."

Shaw listened to Wood's story. Only later would Shaw learn that Wood was nowhere near the potato factory the day his mother died in the fire. He reached over and gripped Wood's hand. "Listen, Jim, things were rough for you," Shaw said, knowing full well that Wood was conning him. "But I need to know about Jeralee. You've said you took her. How did you do it?"

"I seen her when I was over at Liz and Tammy's," said Wood, explaining that he left after the little girl did. When he next saw Jeralee, Wood told her Liz Smith's check would not clear. Then he threw Jeralee into his car and drove south.

"What did you talk about?" Shaw asked. "Did she tell you her name?"

"Uh, she told me her last name was Underwood. I remember right after we left, I was drinking a beer. I offered her one, and she didn't want it. She said she didn't drink, she come from a religious family, and she didn't want a drink. I told her to try it, she might like it. But she said she didn't drink."

"Did you talk about anything else?" Shaw asked.

"She said she was a dancer, she did clogging, and she come from a religious family. She said she was a Mormon, and she asked me what religion I was. I told her I didn't have any particular religion. And right after that, I stopped at a restaurant and a gas station to get some beer."

Wood continued to tell the same story: he put Jeralee out in a field near Preston. Only this time, his story changed slightly. Now it was dark when he let the little paper girl out near the field. "What was her name?" Wood asked. "Oh, Jeralee. Yeah, Jeralee."

"Jim," I've got a problem with the time," Shaw said. "Before, you said it was still daylight when you put her out. Now, it's dark. You took Jeralee at 5:30. You stopped near the willow at the creek, but you didn't stay. Jim, it's an hour and a half, two hours tops, to Preston, so that puts you down there at 7:30 at the latest. But you say it was dark when you let her out. That means it was at least 8:30. I don't think you're telling me the whole thing, Jim. You molested that little girl by the willows, didn't you?"

"I was going to, Scott," Wood said, his voice unnaturally high, his eyes beginning to redden. "When I stopped there by the creek, I put my hand on her butt, but she told me to quit it. She said I was disgusting. So I stopped. I was gonna do it, Scott, but so help me God, I didn't. I swear on my mother's grave, I went on down toward Salt Lake, and I let her out at the field, and I said, 'Don't you worry, darlin', somebody's gonna find you and take you to mamma.' That's the last I seen of her, I swear."

"Jim," Shaw said quietly, "why do you suppose

nobody's found her by now and taken her home to mamma?"

"Well, maybe somebody else got her, cause I swear on my mother's grave, Scott, I let her out in that field, knowing somebody would help her."

Shaw glanced at his watch. It was close to nine. He had caught Wood lying. Wood had admitted that he tried to molest Jeralee. Shaw moved the conversation back to Wood's childhood and his bad luck in life. "How did you come to live in Pocatello, Jim?"

"I had a marriage go bad down in Louisiana," Wood said flatly.

"I'm sorry things haven't worked out for you, Jim," Shaw said sadly, putting his arm on Wood's shoulder. "And now here you are, at a time in your life when you should be enjoying some of life's pleasures, your marriage falls apart, you have to leave your home, the part of the country you'd lived in, and come all the way out here with nothing—no money, no job. Things like that put a lot stress on people, Jim. And I know it builds up and it doesn't go away. It just builds and builds 'til you just want to explode, don't you Jim? I think that's why you took Jeralee."

"Yeah, it does," Wood said quietly, his head in his hands. "It just builds up 'till you want to explode. I just blew up, and I took her."

"Where is she, Jim?"

"I told you," he said, turning to look at Shaw. "I let her off at that field, by that sign that said Bear River."

"Look, Jim," Shaw said solemnly. "I understand what you were going through."

Wood looked at Shaw and placed his hand on the detective's hand. "Scott, it's good to have somebody that understands. I'm glad it was you, I'm glad it was you."

"Jim, I need to know where that little girl is. I need to know."

"I can't tell you," Wood said, putting his elbows in his knees and resting his head in his hand.

"Can't or won't?"

"I can't," Wood said. "If I did, nobody would understand me. They wouldn't understand what I did."

"Jim," Shaw said, "I understand you. I'm not gonna judge you, I won't think any less of you. But I need to know what happened."

Shaw reached over and put his arm on Wood's shoulder. Wood wiped his eyes with the back of his hands.

"If I tell you, you'll think I'm the scum of the earth," he said, beginning to sob. "You won't be nice to me anymore."

"Jim, she's dead, isn't she?"

Wood's hands were in his lap, clenched. He seemed to be making an effort to maintain his composure. He looked straight ahead and took a deep breath. He nodded.

"Jim, I already knew that. Why was it so hard to tell me what happened?"

"Because I'm evil," Wood said, staring up at the

wall behind Shaw's desk. "Because I'm an evil monster and I'm an animal."

"We're going to have to talk about what happened," Shaw said.

Wood nodded. He reached for his package of Marlboros and tapped it. It was empty. Was it possible to get more cigarettes? Shaw said he would send someone for more. He went outside. Standing outside Shaw's office were Chief Benham and several other officers. Everyone was waiting for news.

"She's dead," Shaw told Chief Benham.

As Shaw went back into his office, Chief Benham called Kert Howard, the Underwoods' stake president who was now acting as the family's spokesman. Benham told Howard that Jeralee was dead and asked if Howard would go with him and Captain Lynn Harris to break the news to Jeff and Joyce Underwood. They had already been told that a man suspected of kidnapping Jeralee had been arrested.

The three men arrived at the Underwoods' home just before eleven that night. When Jeff opened the door and saw them, he knew his daughter was not going to return. With Joyce at his side, he waited for the words. Chief Benham said simply, "Jeff, Joyce, this is not how I wanted this to turn out...but Jeralee is no longer with us." The Underwoods held each other and wept silently.

Their five children were already in their bedrooms asleep. The Underwoods decided not to awaken them. They would tell them in the morning.

Kert Howard gave the priesthood blessing to Jeff and Joyce, a blessing of comfort and strength. Jeff would give the blessing to each of their children in the morning after they had been told their sister would not be coming home.

24

When Shaw returned to the office with the cigarettes, Wood no longer seemed upset. Instead, he now appeared calm and relaxed. He smiled when Shaw came into the room. Shaw sat down in the chair beside Wood and began to ask him about Jeralee. But now Wood was reluctant to talk about the little girl. Once again, Shaw steered the conversation back to Wood's troubled life, then brought it back to Jeralee. Shaw assured Wood that he understood why he killed Jeralee, that he would not judge Wood for what he had done.

After several minutes, Wood was willing to tell Shaw more about what happened in the hours after he forced Jeralee into his car. After turning east toward Preston, Wood said, he drove around "all night," finally parking in a "circle" near a subdivision just before daybreak. Based on the description of the subdivision and a convenience store, Shaw knew Wood and Jeralee had been in Preston. Wood said he parked in the "circle," locked the doors from the inside, then passed out. The little girl slept, too, and did not try to escape.

Later that morning, said Wood, he woke up just at dawn. "There were cars still driving with their headlights on, but it was light enough to see the cars. So I just started up and come on back this way, come back toward Pocatello. But I seen this little lean-to building in a farmer's field near the river. So I pulled down there, and there was, was people fishing down there, so I come on outta there. And there was people on the other side of the river fishin', on both sides. I just kept on comin' back to Pocatello. Drove right through Pocatello."

"Did you try to molest her there by the river, Jim?"

"No, I'm tellin' the truth, I'm spilling it, so help me, Scott, I didn't touch her. I wanted to, but I couldn't. So I just come on back to Pocatello. I was gonna bring her home, but I panicked, so help me God. I'd been with that little girl so long, she could identify me. I drove right on down Yellowstone, come on past the house, and didn't see nobody, so I just drove on out the old highway. I was just driving and driving, and I ended up in Idaho Falls.

As he talked, Wood began to appear highly agitated.

"And I pulled in by the river, and all the stress was building," Wood said. "And the little girl said she had to go pee, so I said, 'you go on,' and I got her

out and walked her up this little knoll, and she
pulled her panties down and squatted down, and I
shot her. But she didn't feel it, Scott. She didn't feel
a thing."

Shaw could hardly believe Wood's implication
that since the child had felt no pain, all had turned
out OK in the end. "Where'd you shoot her, Jim?"

"In the head."

"Once, twice?"

"Twice," Wood said.

Shaw paused for a moment. For the first time
since he had started talking to Wood, he felt an
almost uncontrollable anger toward the man sitting
by his side. But if Shaw showed anger or any emotion at all, he was sure Wood would shut down.
Calmly, he asked where Wood left the body.

"It was right there on the river...I don't exactly
remember where...but she didn't feel no pain, no
sir."

"Jim, it's very important you tell me exactly
where you left her."

"I swear, Scott, I can't say...I'm tellin' the truth, I
just don't know...I just know I'm sick. I'm sick, and
I need some kinda help, and that's the honest truth."

"Have you got any kids, Jim?" Shaw asked.

"Yes," said Wood. "I got three."

"Well, if somebody shot one of them, wouldn't
you want to know where they were? Wouldn't you
want to know where your child was, Jim?" Shaw said
softly.

Wood turned and looked at Shaw, showing no
emotion at all. "How can you just sit there and act

so calm when we're talking about things like this?" he asked Shaw. And then Wood shut down, as though a wall had gone up around his mind. He would not go any further.

Shaw tried a different approach. But he knew immediately he had made a mistake. "Jim, what would you do if I told you we've already found the body?"

Wood stood up. As he did, his chair slid backward across the tile floor of Shaw's office. "I'd say you're damned wrong," he said coldly, his eyes now hard and cold as he glared at his interrogator.

Shaw had tried to bluff Wood by saying the body had been found and he had been caught. It would be almost half an hour before Shaw knew why Wood had been so sure he had been bluffing. But for now, Wood again refused to say anything else about Jeralee.

As he had several times before, Shaw began slowly building Wood's trust by guiding the conversation back to Wood's troubled life. Soon Wood began to talk about his mother's death and the woman in gray who pushed him away when he wanted to rescue his mother. Shaw listened and began to press Wood for more information on where he had left Jeralee's body.

"Jim, I need to know. Where on the river in Idaho Falls did you leave her?"

"Scott, it was just a blur," Wood said, tapping cigarette ashes into the Coke can. "I just don't remember, I swear to God, I just don't remember," he said in a child-like voice.

"Jim, you don't shoot somebody in the head twice and forget it," Shaw said.

Suddenly Wood began to sob, his shoulders heaving. He buried his face in his hands. Shaw put his hand on Wood's shoulder and patted gently.

"I know what you must've been going through, Jim," Shaw said. "But you need to tell me about it." Shaw was well aware that Wood's show of emotion was a total ruse. Wood was only acting the way the situation demanded.

"I can't tell you," Wood said. "If I do, you won't have any respect for me," he sobbed. "Nobody will. I won't have nobody to talk to, and I don't know what I'd do if I didn't have somebody I could talk to."

"Jim, I told you when we first came in we had a lot of things to work though. I know you were under stress, Jim. I know you weren't responsible for what happened."

"I'm a monster," Wood sobbed. "I'm evil, I ain't nothing but an animal!"

"Jim."

"Scott," Wood said, turning toward Shaw, looking into his eyes. "Scott, I swear, I'm in Satan's grip. I've got demons in me, and if I tell you some things, I'm scared one will leave me and go into you!"

Shaw assured Wood he was safe from demons. "But you'll feel better if you tell me everything. Just go ahead and get it off your chest," Shaw said, putting his hand on Wood's. "I know you remember where you left that little girl. Jim, I need to know where she is."

Wood sniffled but said nothing.

"Jim," Shaw said, "you didn't cry when you told me you shot her, so why is this so hard?"

Suddenly, Wood's expression changed. He looked ahead toward the wall behind Shaw's desk. Then he turned and looked at Shaw. "I threw her in the river," he said flatly.

"You shot her and you threw her in the river?" Shaw asked.

"No...Scott, I don't know...I went on back up there today," Wood said calmly. "I cut her up."

Shaw tried hard to not show any reaction to what Wood had just said. "How did you cut her up?"

"I took a little camp ax, and a mountain knife...I cut her up. I just threw her in the river there."

"Did you throw her clothing in the river, too?"

"Yep."

"What about your clothes? Did you have blood on you?"

"I had a T-shirt on. I went down to the river and washed my hands and throwed my T-shirt and cut-offs in the river. I put on my other pair of jeans and another T-shirt and tennis shoes, and I come on back to Pocatello."

"Jim, you're holding something back here," Shaw persisted. "What else is there you need to tell me? We've been honest here, and you've told me things, but you need to tell me everything."

"I had sex with her when I went back up there," Wood said, looking at Shaw.

"What do you mean?"

"After I shot her," Wood said, his voice breaking,

sobbing, sniffing. "I just covered her up with some bushes. And when I went back up there this mornin', I uncovered her, and I had sex with her. I just rolled her over and took off her clothes and did it. But I didn't finish...there was ants and things crawling on her, I couldn't finish doing it. I was throwing up the whole time."

Shaw took a deep breath and sat back in his chair.

Wood was finished. He stopped crying and looked at Shaw. "This was hard on me," Wood said, placing his hand on Shaw's.

"I know it was, Jim," Shaw said. It was time for a break. Shaw had to go outside and tell Chief Benham what he had heard. "Are you ready for another Coke?" he asked Wood.

Wood smiled. "Yeah," he said. "I've been talking quite a bit. My mouth's gettin' a little dry."

Shaw left Wood in his office while he stepped outside. Chief Benham had returned from visiting the Underwoods and was standing outside with the other officers who still gathered near Shaw's office. Shaw told the officers that Wood dismembered Jeralee's body in Idaho Falls and threw her in the Snake River. Wood had agreed to go with Shaw to Idaho Falls to show him the location. Arrangements were made to notify the police in Idaho Falls, and a call was placed to FBI headquarters in Washington, D.C. The forensic team that had been placed on standby was told that the crime scene was in Idaho Falls.

Shaw was emotionally drained, but there was more to do. He had to get Wood's statement on tape.

Before taping the session, he asked Detective Brennan to go to the Arctic Circle on Yellowstone Avenue to get hamburgers, fries, and sodas for Wood and himself. They ate in Shaw's office and talked about fishing, to maintain Wood's confidence.

When they finished, Shaw placed the cassette recorder on his desk. Wood repeated what he had said earlier. It was close to eleven when the taped session began. It was close to three in the morning when it ended.

Next, in the predawn darkness, Shaw and Detective Scott Marchand led Wood to a patrol car so he could lead them to the place where Jeralee had died. As they drove north on a deserted Yellowstone Avenue, followed by Chief Benham's car and several others, Shaw asked Wood what he had done with the gun he'd used to kill Jeralee. The .22 Jennings was not found in the search of Dave Haggard's property or Wood's car. Wood said he hid it beside a small road near Chubbuck. He did not know the name of the road but said he could find it. As they continued down Yellowstone Avenue, they passed the Subway shop.

"Did you rob the Subway a few months back?" Shaw asked.

"Yeah, that was me," Wood said.

Soon they crossed Interstate 86 and drove into Chubbuck. Following Wood's directions, the driver, Detective Marchand, turned onto Reservation Road. It led into dark, open fields. Soon they reached Hill Line Road, a small, two-lane, gravel country road. "Take a right here," Wood said. "Now pull over."

With the headlights shining into the darkness, Wood pointed to a large sagebrush a few feet from the road. The gun was under the sagebrush, Wood said, wrapped in a scarf.

While Marchand took his flashlight and got out, Shaw remained in the car with Wood. In a moment, Marchand came back to the car. "It's where he said it was." Shaw got out and looked beneath the sagebrush. In the light from the headlights, he saw what appeared to be a small bundle wrapped in cloth. An evidence technician arrived to photograph the gun in its location before it was retrieved.

With Marchand's car leading the way, the caravan went north on Hill Line Road until they reached Interstate 15. Soon they accelerated to interstate speeds, traveling north toward Idaho Falls. Wood, seated in the back of the patrol car with Shaw, began to talk about his childhood in Idaho Falls. The place by the river where he murdered Jeralee had been a favorite fishing spot when Wood was a young boy. The road to Idaho Falls, he said later, reminded him of the time he spent at the youth correction center in St. Anthony, about thirty miles above Idaho Falls. He told Shaw he had driven to St. Anthony recently to see the place where he was confined for most of his teenage years.

"It looked pretty much the same as I remember," Wood said.

As they drove on through the night, the officers passed through the eastern edge of an 800-square-mile lava field, one of many that dot the Snake River Plain. There, the rich soil of the plain gave way to a huge field of dark basalt, frozen forever in bizarre shapes when the molten rock cooled more than 2,000 years ago. Over time, windblown soil collected in the cracks and crevices of the rock. Now juniper trees were scattered across the surface of the foreboding landscape, as though they had taken root in the rock itself. The lava field was a strange, desolate, windblown place. When the early pioneers first saw it, they named it Hell's Half Acre. On that early morning on the last day of June when Wood's Buick Century passed through the lava field on its way to Idaho Falls, for Jeralee, the place truly was hell on earth.

Wood directed Marchand to take the airport exit in Idaho Falls. They turned onto a small paved access road that ran past a small café. Wood told Marchand to take a small dirt road leading to the river. The narrow dirt road crossed a small wooden bridge over an irrigation canal. As the road fed into a dusty parking area, Wood told Marchand to stop.

"See that path down to the river?" Wood asked.

In the tunnels of the headlights, Shaw saw a break in the tall brown weeds where the path began. "I see it," said Shaw.

"Now, see that little knoll there to the left?" Wood asked. Shaw could see where the tall, brown grass rose higher than the rest. At the top of the rise was a large, dead sagebrush surrounded by thick scrub brush.

Taking his flashlight, Shaw jumped out of the patrol car and walked toward the break, staying to the side of the footpath so he would not disturb the footprints he could see on the dusty trail. Blackness closed in on him as he walked further into the tall grass. Now he played the bright beam from his flashlight ahead of him.

Holding onto scrub brush, Shaw pulled himself up the rise. He aimed the light around the small clearing, now only a yard or two from where he stood. The dry grass surrounding the clearing had been pressed down, as though an animal had bedded down. Shaw noticed the soil was moist with a dark, thick liquid. There were chop marks, presumably from the axe, in the ground. Small pieces of tissue and white bone protruded from some of the chop marks. A nearby stump was coated in blood.

Shaw stood motionless as the beam of light fell on the small clearing. He was only yards from the river now. He could hear the sound of the cold, black waters of the Snake River rushing past in the darkness.

Back at the clearing, Shaw told the other officers what he had seen. The crime scene was sealed by units from the Idaho Falls Police Department and the Bonneville County Sheriff's Department.

Shaw went back to Marchand's car and sat down beside Wood. He said nothing. Soon they were back on the interstate driving back to Pocatello.

The first gray of dawn appeared over the eastern foothills as Marchand pulled into the parking lot behind the station. Shaw and Marchand walked on either side of James Wood, who still wore the same jeans and pullover he had on when he was arrested. Inside, Wood was processed—fingerprints were taken and photographs made—and he was readied to be transported to the Bannock County Jail.

Shaw watched as Wood was escorted by officers toward the stairwell, his arms cuffed behind his back. As the officers led him toward the stairwell door, Wood looked back at Shaw and gave a him a weak smile.

It was after six when Shaw returned to his small office and sat down behind his desk. The arraignment was scheduled for one-thirty in the afternoon, so the report of Wood's arrest and statements had to be completed. Shaw stared at the forms in front of him for what to him seemed an eternity. Where to begin? Unable to concentrate, Shaw walked outside to clear his head.

Chief Benham, who had just returned from Idaho Falls, saw Shaw standing outside his office. "Shaw," he said quietly, "Go home and get some sleep."

Shaw got his jacket and went outside. The morning air still felt cool as he walked to his patrol car and started home. As he turned into his driveway, Shaw suddenly realized that he had taken his official car home, a transgression strictly forbidden under departmental policy. He had left his Bronco parked behind the station.

Inside, Shaw walked upstairs to the hallway and opened the door to Krissy's room. Seeing she was asleep, he sat on the edge of her bed and watched her for a moment. Then he went down the hall to his bedroom and fell asleep.

Shaw awoke less than three hours later. Vonny had left for work and Krissy and Jason had gone to school. The house was quiet as he showered and dressed for work.

As he neared the subdivision where the Underwoods lived, he slowed and signaled for a left turn. Shaw went to the door and knocked. Kert Howard, the stake president, opened the door.

As Shaw came in, his eyes meet those of Jeff and Joyce. Shaw stood for a moment. "I'm sorry," he said. "We were just too late."

Jeff and Joyce Underwood approached Shaw. In silence, the three embraced.

25

Meantime, in Idaho Falls, a grim search was underway. Shallow-draft aluminum jet boats of the Bonneville County Sheriff's Department search team had begun the search for Jeralee's remains. Earlier, a boat carrying a dog named Duke and his handler had cruised upstream near the western bank. Duke was trained to smell human remains, even in water. The animal became extremely agitated as the boat cruised close to the bank several hundred yards below where Jeralee had died. At one point, the scent was so strong, the dog had to be restrained from jumping into the water.

The search concentrated along the stretch of the river where the scent had been strongest. When the silver boats throttled back and maneuvered against the current to stay in position, divers clad in orange-and-black suits dropped into the cold, swift waters.

Other men fought the strong current as they waded in waist-deep water along the brush-covered western shore of the river. Spectators gathered on the silver railroad trestle that spanned the wide river. Overhead, a news helicopter from a Salt Lake City television station circled the scene.

First to be found was a man's thong, almost 600 yards down river from where Jeralee was killed. It was later determined that it belonged to James Wood. Just before eleven-thirty on this windy, sunny morning, Jeralee's *Idaho State Journal* canvas newspaper bag was pulled from the water. It had been weighted down with sand and rocks. Then, scattered along a 200-yard stretch of the river, the remains of Jeralee Underwood were recovered from the cold waters.

Later that day, Detective Shaw spoke with authorities in Bridgeton, Missouri. Shaw learned that Wood's victim in the Missouri shooting had survived. Her name was Jeanne Faser. Originally, her boyfriend had been a suspect. The case had remained unsolved until the call came from Shaw.

Next, Shaw placed a call to authorities in Caddo Parish, Louisiana. Wood's confession cleared a case that had baffled investigators in Caddo Parish for almost two decades. On Christmas Eve in 1976, Shirley Coleman, a thirty-three year-old Shreveport mother of four, disappeared while Christmas shopping. Her skeleton—along with a leather coat, a shoe, and a bra—were found in the woods by hunters five years later. There was a small-caliber bullet hole in the back of her skull.

Across town, Jeff Underwood issued a statement through Stake President Kert Howard, who continued to act as the family's spokesman. The Underwoods thanked the community and the media for all the support they had received.

"There has been shock and a lot of tears shed," Howard explained. "They feel their prayers were answered. The family prayed for an answer to what happened to their daughter, and they got the answer. There is no vindication on the part of Jeff and Joyce Underwood. They just want justice done, but there is no talk of revenge.

"They believe that on Resurrection Day, her body and spirit will be reunited whole and perfect. They know that the body just houses the spirit and that Jeralee's spirit was unhurt. That belief has helped them through this. They have the strongest faith of any family in our stake, and it has gotten them through this.

"Jeff is not a tall man," Howard added. "But he is a giant in his faith and his spirit."

Shortly after news of James Wood's arrest for the murder of Jeralee Underwood was announced, reporters and camera crews converged on Dave Haggard's house. Neighbors watched as a parade of cars and trucks drove slowly past Haggard's home. Curious onlookers came from as far away as Idaho Falls to see the house where the killer had lived. Wood's offense was now being called the most brutal crime in modern Idaho history.

A photograph of Haggard appeared on the front page of the *Idaho State Journal.* Haggard, wearing a baseball hat and smiling toward the camera, was seated in a rocking chair in his den. Behind him was the huge mural painted by Wood shortly after he arrived in Pocatello.

Liz Smith and Tammy Retzlof were also sought out by reporters and camera crews. Liz vehemently denied reports that she was related to James Wood. "I'm not his aunt!" she snapped, referring to false reports that had appeared in the newspaper and on television.

One day after learning their oldest daughter had been killed, Jeff and Joyce Underwood decided to hold a press conference at the Stake Center on Grant Street. "We felt a need to personally respond to the outpouring of kindness," they said.

Standing before a wooden table with a framed portrait of Jeralee and a copy of the Book of Mormon, Jeff and Joyce were introduced to dozens of reporters and camera crews crowded before them. Jeff stepped up to a forest of microphones attached to the dais. Holding Joyce tightly by his side, he looked into the bright lights of the cameras. "Our Heavenly Father has heard everyone's prayers and brought our daughter back to us. We now know where she is," he said, his voice breaking. "The Lord performed a miracle by catching the person who did this to us."

But it was shy, pretty Joyce who brought tears to

the eyes of many in the room. She was asked about the media reports of animosity in the community and threats on Wood's life.

"I've learned a lot about love this week," Joyce said, close to tears. "And I also know there is a lot of hate. I've looked at the love, and I've felt the love, and I want to continue feeling the love. Jeralee would always forgive people who hurt her," Joyce said quietly. "She would think of things she could do to go back and love that person. We can forgive."

The next morning under a bright summer sky, Jeralee was buried. More than 1,000 mourners filled the chapel at the Stake Center while hundreds more watched a closed-circuit transmission of the service at the Latter-day Saints' chapel on the Old Bannock Highway.

A wall of wreaths, many with pink flowers and pink ribbons, surrounded Jeralee's small coffin. Jeralee's cousins, many of whom she had met for the first time at a family reunion in Boise only two weeks earlier, sang "I Am a Child of God." A children's chorus sang other hymns.

The church authority was represented by Elder James Faust of the Council of Twelve and Elder Joe J. Christensen of the Council of Seventy. Elder Faust read a letter from the first presidency, then spoke to Jeff and Joyce and their five children. "It has not been my privilege to know Jeralee. But as I have observed the happenings in these eleven days, I believe that in her short being she has literally changed the lives of others more than many do in a whole lifetime," remarked Elder Faust.

When the service ended, the funeral procession wound its way through the working class neighborhoods near the Stake Center on its way to the cemetery. As the white hearse slowly moved past, onlookers lined the streets.

26

The days and weeks following Wood's arrest passed in a blur for Scott Shaw. In addition to tedious and time-consuming reports that had to be written, Shaw also was swamped by inquires from law enforcement agencies around the country. Special attention was given to cases in areas where Wood was known to have lived or traveled. Even cases that had been inactive for decades were reviewed for similarities to Wood's method of assault.

Throughout his adult life, Wood had often worked as a truck driver. When he was married and living in Florrisant, Missouri, he had worked for two trucking companies and had traveled throughout the South and Southwest. In Louisiana in the late 1970s, Wood drove an oil delivery truck. Following his release from Angola in 1986, he was a truck driver for a carnival based in Tyler, Texas. His work took him to Louisiana, Oklahoma, and Texas. Three un-solved cases near Shreveport, where Wood lived from 1978 until late 1979, closely matched Wood's modus operandi. All involved young women who either disappeared or were found murdered.

In the summer of 1978, an attractive twenty-five-year-old artist and part-time real estate agent, Bo Bo Shin, disappeared in Magnolia, Arkansas. She disap-peared after telling friends she was going to show a home to a prospective buyer. Her car was later found abandoned at a shopping center. Shin was never seen again. A police composite of a man seen talking with Shin in the parking lot shortly before she disappeared looked remarkably like Wood. Mag-nolia was only ninety minutes north of Bossier Par-ish, Louisiana, where Wood lived. Wood was driving the oil rig and teaching art classes at the time.

On March 15, 1979, a Louisiana woman in her early twenties named Aurilla Vaul disappeared after dropping off her husband at work and driving to nearby Bossier Parish. Her car was later found, but Vaul has not been seen since.

The youngest of the three victims was eighteen-year-old Ladoisha "Dottie" Gay. Her car was found in the parking lot of the Eastgate Shopping Center in Shreveport in 1979. Six weeks later, the teenager's body was discovered in a wooded area near a high-way in northwestern Louisiana.

Back in Pocatello, for the next six months James Wood disregarded the advice of his court-appointed public defender and met almost daily with Detective Shaw. On days when Shaw did not come to the Bannock County Jail, Wood often phoned the detective from the pay phone in his small, isolated cell, inviting Shaw to "come over for a chat." Soon the sight of Shaw arriving at the jail, carrying a sack of fast food for the most infamous killer in Idaho history, attracted the interest of the press and curious others. Much was made of the strange relationship that seemed to have formed between the two men.

For his part, Shaw was both repulsed and fascinated by Wood. On one level, he found Wood repugnant. On another level, Wood presented an opportunity few law enforcement professionals would ever have—the chance to probe the mind of a true sociopath.

Listening day after day as Wood discussed topics ranging from his troubled childhood to his violent sexual fantasies and unimaginably brutal crimes, Shaw began to pay an emotional price. Most of Wood's sexual crimes involved children. Shaw's children were the center of his life. A year earlier, his oldest son, Scott Jr., now a Bannock County sheriff's deputy, had moved into an apartment of his own. Almost every evening at home, Shaw stopped and peered into Scott Jr.'s old room.

"I just felt lonely and sad that he wasn't home. I can't walk in and talk to him, or just know he's home and safe where he belongs," Shaw told a friend. "It would be devastating if something happened to one of mine. Yet I had to hide my feelings from the moment I met James Wood until the day he left for Boise."

Still, during those six months before Wood was transferred to the Idaho State Penitentiary in Boise, Wood opened up to Shaw more than he ever had to anyone in his life. The "most hated man in Idaho" told his life story.

By Wood's own estimation, from the time he was eighteen years old until he was arrested in Po-catello—a period spanning three decades—he committed at least eighty-five rapes and perhaps more than 185 armed robberies.

His first brush with the law took place when he was six years old. While playing on an iced-over part of the Snake River in Idaho Falls, he refused a policeman's request to get off the ice. He was rescued by the fire department.

By age nine, Wood had experienced a "very strong" sexual fantasy that stayed with him. It involved the violent rape of a classmate in elementary school. Wood did not like the little girl because "she was pretty and her family had a lot of money."

When he was fourteen, Wood stole a car and was placed on probation. Later that same year, he ran away from his aunt and uncle's home in Idaho Falls and was caught setting fire to dumpsters in Pocatello. Mildred and Gene Wood, who had adopted the boy following his mother's death in the fire at the potato processing plant, told authorities they did not want Wood returned to their home. Wood became a ward of the state. As a result, Wood spent most of his teenage years at St. Anthony's Youth Correction

Center, a forlorn institution on the Snake River Plain near St. Anthony, Idaho. During three incarcerations at St. Anthony's, Wood took part in at least seven escape attempts. During one successful attempt involving several other youths whom Wood organized, he held a knife to the throat of a guard and threatened to kill him. When he was seventeen, he was released from St. Anthony's and went to live with his biological father who had recently been released from federal prison and lived in Louisiana.

Wood raped his first victim when he was twenty-two. Within hours, he raped his second victim in Bellview, Illinois. She "resisted," so Wood "hit her very hard in the face" and began to "choke her" until she complied with his demands. Afterward, Wood shoved the naked woman out of his car and threw her clothing and purse in the Missouri River.

Following two arrests as an adult, Wood spent almost one-quarter of his life behind bars during two terms at Louisiana's infamous Angola prison. Still, he managed to marry three times and to father three children. He also had opportunistic homosexual relationships throughout his life. He crossed gender lines if it meant getting money or protection.

The first living thing he ever killed, Wood said, was a colt. He was nineteen and had just left his first wife. Wood was spending the Christmas holidays in Arkansas with the parents of a man with whom he had a homosexual relationship. On Christmas Eve, Wood took a shotgun belonging to the father of his friend and went for a walk in the woods. He came upon a colt tied to a tree in a pine thicket. The colt was apparently a Christmas present for the children of a family living nearby and was being hidden until Christmas morning. Wood shot the colt at close range with the shotgun, "just to see what it felt like to kill something."

Wood admitted to three murders—that of Jeralee Underwood, a Missouri teenager, and a woman in Louisiana. The Louisiana victim was a young mother of four, thirty-three-year-old Shirly Coleman of Shreveport. Wood abducted her from a parking lot on Christmas Eve in 1976.

"I didn't have any place to go, so I figured I'd have myself a little party," Wood recalled. "I waited and watched this woman. She had a nice car and just looked like she had money. I'd never been around a woman like that. She was sophisticated, and she had class. All the girls I'd had were cheap. I just thought, by God, I'm going to have some of that."

"So your fantasy is making love with a classy lady and having her love you?" Shaw asked.

"Yeah, Scott. Something like that."

"What about the girl you abducted at the Pizza Hut here in Pocatello?"

"The girl at the Pizza Hut was different. She just looked like the all-American girl. Not too pretty, not too plain, just average. But she did look like somebody with a good life. Nothing to worry about."

"You mean she looked innocent?"

"Yeah," Wood said. "Innocent. The kind of girl I wished I could've dated. So took her on a date."

"Is a *date* something you think about all the time?"

"Yeah, it is."

"How hard, or how much, do you think about it?"

"When the mood strikes."

"Tell me about the girl at the Pizza Hut."

"Well, I was just leaving, and there she was. She was carrying a baby and getting into a car. I just walked over there and showed her my gun and told her to get on over. I could tell she was so scared she couldn't think straight. I drove around just thinking about what I was going to do and had a hard time finding some place to park. When I did, I had her put the baby in the back seat and had her sit over by me. I kissed her a little and played with her boobies. Then I had her pants off and licked her a little bit. Everything was going so well I just popped off before we got to the good stuff. That didn't stop me, though, 'cause I just kept going and screwed her anyway."

"Were you fantasizing before you climaxed?" Shaw asked.

"Yeah, I guess you could say that."

"Then what?"

"When I was done, I had her get out of the car. I walked her over to some bushes. I had her kneel down, and I took my pistol out and tried to shoot her in the head. The fucking thing didn't go off. I was too close to the road and some houses to fuck around and find the shell casings. If I'd jacked another round in the chamber, I'd had two of them to look for. I knew I didn't have time to do that after I shot her. I would've had to shoot the baby, too, and that would've took more time. God really watched out for her that day."

"How did you manage to control her?" Shaw
asked. "Didn't anybody you ever had in the car with
you try to get away, try to attract attention?"

"It was the gun," said Wood. "Once I showed it,
I usually didn't have to get it out again. If they
started acting like they didn't want to do what I told
them to, all I had to do was this," he said, patting his
waistband where he always placed the gun.

"Still, there must've been some time that somebody didn't do exactly what you told them to," Shaw
persisted. "Didn't anybody ever try to resist?"

"Once in a while, maybe, somebody would act
up," Wood said, pausing to take a drag from his
cigarette. "But once they saw the eye of the beast,
they always came around. They'd do what I said."

Shaw did not doubt it for a second. During their
conversations, he had seen the rage in Wood's eyes
when Shaw pressed him on issues Wood did not
want to discuss. When Wood became angry, his
entire countenance changed. His face hardened. The
rage seemed to emerge from deep inside, something
so evil, so primal, that it caused the hairs on Shaw's
neck to stand on end. Shaw had often pondered the
possibility of photographing Wood in this state. If
such a photo were compared to a regular picture of
Wood, he doubted that anyone would recognize the
man.

When Shaw brought up the shooting of the Missouri teenager, seventeen-year-old Jeanne Faser, he
noticed an expression of surprise register on Wood's
face. Wood believed he had killed Jeanne until Shaw
told him that the teenager had survived.

"I'm real surprised to hear that," he told Shaw.

In earlier conversations with Shaw, Wood had proved evasive when the detective tried to get him to discuss Jeralee's death and the acts Wood performed on her body later. Wood only said that what happened to Jeralee was "as far as I could go."

"That doesn't tell me anything, Jim. I want you to explain exactly what you mean," Shaw insisted.

Finally, Wood explained himself. "When she came in to collect for Liz's paper, I told her she could be president one day. She was on her own paper route, and she was talking to everybody. There was nothing stopping her from doing whatever she wanted to do."

"Did that make you mad?"

"No, I wanted it."

"Wanted what?"

"I wanted to have her."

"What do you mean, 'have her'? To own her? Possess her?"

"Kinda. And it made me mad."

"Why did it make you mad?" Shaw asked.

"Well, not really mad," Wood said, taking a draw on his cigarette. "I just wanted her. Wanted to use her all up. I just wanted to be with her and use her all up."

"Just because you thought she could be president?"

"She was just so innocent," Wood said, looking upward toward the patch of sky above the jail's exercise yard. "Hell, probably nobody ever said 'boo' to her, I'll bet."

"We're back to *innocence* now, Jim. Why does that turn you on?"

"I don't know. I just want to rub it all over me and have some of it. Maybe I can keep it."

"So you're saying everything you've done in your life culminated with that little girl?"

"I'm saying I went as far as I could because there's nothing else I could do that would ever beat it."

"Are you saying you've run out of fantasies and your last one was Jeralee?"

"Yes," Wood said. Finally, he disclosed how he had mutilated the child's body and later returned to have sex with her corpse. "And I liked it, Scott," Wood said earnestly, looking at Shaw. "I'm some kinda monster, because it gave me peace."

Shaw was sick to his stomach but continued his questions, trying not to show emotion. "Was it the mother of all fantasies? I mean, did you finally get it right?"

"I just felt like I had to do it. Kinda like needing a cigarette, only a thousand times worse."

"If you compare it to needing a cigarette, you're saying you'll need more cigarettes."

"No doubt about it, Scott. No doubt at all."

But as the days passed and the conversations continued, Shaw was convinced Wood had been responsible for more homicides. After all, Wood's first admitted killing took place in 1976 in Louisiana. According to Wood, Jeralee was his second murder victim. But Shaw knew better. Although serial killers often have a "cooling off" period between crimes, a period of more than seventeen years was unlikely.

Still, in their ongoing jailhouse meetings, Wood continued to deny he had killed anyone other than Shirley Coleman and Jeralee Underwood. But one day, Wood finally hinted at what Shaw had thought all along. Wood had most likely committed numerous other murders. As Shaw pressed for answers, Wood became angry. Then, Wood composed himself, smiled and said simply, "I'll tell you one day."

Shortly after that meeting, Shaw wondered if Wood, in his own way, was providing him with an answer to his question about other murders. Wood gave Shaw a self-portrait done in pencil. Within the profile of Wood's face, a small figure, like that of a little girl, appeared to be fleeing. She cast a long shadow behind her. At the top of the drawing, Wood had sketched a cross and the scales of justice. Atop the scales he'd written, in his neat, stylized handwriting, the Biblical quote, "Where sin abounds, God's Grace abounds much more thereof."

Finally, a disturbing, ghostly image of a woman in a long, flowing robe, dominated the lower corner of the sketch. She appeared to hold a knife. Behind her, other, smaller ghostly apparitions receded into the dark background. These figures, Wood told Shaw, represented his victims.

Shaw counted some sixty images.

Epilogue

Regardless of the number of crimes Wood may have committed, he was officially charged with fourteen crimes, including the kidnapping and murder of Jeralee Underwood and the rapes of Beth Edwards and Karen Davis. Wood plead guilty to the murder and rape charges.

On a cold winter morning in December 1993, spectators crowded into Pocatello's Bancock County courthouse for Wood's sentencing hearing. Among those in the courtroom were Jeff and Joyce Underwood. It was the first time they had seen the man who had murdered their daughter.

Among those who had testified at the sentencing hearing was Dr. Vickie R. Gregory, a psychologist from Salt Lake City, who had been appointed by the prosecution to evaluate Wood. Although she found Wood to be legally sane, she believed he posed "an extreme danger to the public." Gregory also cited an evaluation of Wood when he was only sixteen that described him as displaying "evasiveness, defensiveness, and having difficulty with logic and judgment." Gregory explained that "the extreme rage found in such individuals, combined with their sensitivity to criticism and suspicious nature, often leads to unpredictable and irrational violent outbursts."

Gregory also cited other evaluations of Wood which had been made when he was an inmate at Angola State Penitentiary. Those evaluations matched her own—Wood showed signs of sexual sadism, anti-social disorders and compulsiveness. He had little regard for the truth and lacked remorse. In kidnapping Jeralee, Gregory believed Wood acted on impulse.

In her opinion, he could go only for relatively short periods of time without committing a crime.

Another notable witness at the hearing was Jeanne Faser, now nineteen years old, the teenager Wood had shot in the head and left for dead in Missouri. She followed the testimony of Beth Edwards, the teenager Wood had abducted from the Pizza Hut parking lot.

Wearing a metal brace on her right leg, Jeanne walked with a noticeable limp as her mother helped her to the witness stand. She glared at Wood, seated at the defense table, and rarely took her eyes off him during her testimony.

Her voice choking with emotion, the dark-haired young woman told the rapt audience how Wood had abducted her from the gas station, then raped and shot her. The wound had left her deaf in one ear

and partially blind in the left eye. Paralyzed on the
right side, she also suffered from seizures, a speech
impediment and long-term memory loss. The dis-
abilities, Jeanne explained to the hushed courtroom,
were permanent. Fragments from the bullet remained in her brain.

She lay in a coma for three weeks after the
shooting. Her boyfriend, had been arrested by
Bridgeton police for the shooting. He remained in
jail for 35 days before Jeanne was able to speak and
clear him.

After Wood led her into the field after raping her,
Jeanne said, Wood had a "smirk" on his face as he
aimed the pistol at her head. Just before Wood
pulled the trigger, Jeanne said, "he told me 'It's time
to say good-night.' "

"I can tell you what he had on," Jeanne said,
looking directly at Wood, who held his head down,
refusing to make eye contact. "I can tell you what he
smelled like. I can tell you anything about that gentleman that day, and when I say gentleman, I don't
mean nice."

After prosecutor Mark Hiedeman had called the
last witness for the state, Wood had an opportunity
to address the court. He rose from the defense table.
"I've found God," Wood said, "And by the grace of
God, those two girls are alive to testify against me."

Then, Hiedeman, in closing his remarks, read a
list of Wood's crimes. Looking directly at Wood he
said, "We have lost perhaps forever that sense of
small-town innocence. The only way to make it ab-

solutely certain this will never happen again is to impose the death penalty."

On January 14, 1994, just more than a month after the sentencing hearing, Judge Lynn Winmill handed down his decision—James Edward Wood was to die by lethal injection. Wood sat motionless as the sentence was read.

After the announcement, Wood was ordered from the Bancock County Jail to the Idaho State Prison in Boise.

Jeff and Joyce Underwood cried when Judge Winmill read an account of Jeralee's murder before announcing his sentence. When the hearing ended, Jeff and Joyce faced reporters in the corridor.

One reporter asked Joyce Underwood if she agreed with Wood's sentence.

"When we do something wrong," Joyce said, "we need to pay for that. God loves us all, but he doesn't love everything we do."

Wood's public defender, Monte Whittier, spoke to reporters after the hearing. He related a message from Wood "to the people of Pocatello," saying that Wood "felt remorse" and hoped the sentence would "put an end to the hatred" in the community. Whittier added that Wood had hinted that he would not fight the death penalty.

Not only did the Wood case shock Mormons in Pocatello, where 60 percent of the population is Mormon, but in days to come, virtually the entire Church of the Later Day Saints (LDS), in Salt Lake

City, was pulled into controversy. Again, it seemed Wood had been a master manipulator, this time manipulating an entire church.

Within twenty-four hours of his arrest, Wood, a baptized member of the Church of the Later Day Saints, declared his salvation, saying he had 'found God.' During interviews with Scott Shaw, Wood had told the detective that in order to be truly forgiven for his transgressions, he had to allow his life to be taken. Accordingly, he would not appeal his death sentence. Wood, scriptures in hand, echoed passages alluding to "blood atonement," reciting Genesis 9:6, "For whosoever sheds man's blood, By man his blood shall be shed."

Soon after, Wood asked for a meeting with representatives of the Mormon Church. Wood wanted spiritual help. Wood's wishes were granted, and among those attending the meeting with Wood was The LDS stake president.

Shortly after the meeting, Wood dismissed Monte Whittier, his public defender, and obtained a new attorney. Now, he wanted to appeal his death sentence, claiming that during the private meeting with church advisors he was coerced into confessing and that the Mormon Church had planted the idea of "blood atonement" in his mind, saying that his execution would affect his "status in eternity."

Wood also said his sentence was tainted with community and judicial bias since his defense attorney and the presiding judge were both Mormons.

Therefore, Wood insisted, he did not originally fought the death penalty.

Regardless of the fact that the LDS Church has no doctrine on blood atonement, Wood's attorney wanted Mormon officials to disclose the contents of their private temple ceremonies. Church leaders responded by sending their attorneys to Boise to defend against Wood's charges.

On September 12, 1997, the Idaho Supreme Court ruled against Wood, and affirmed his death sentence.

The emotional wounds inflicted on residents of Pocatello, Idaho continue to heal. The Underwoods have moved forward with raising their family, but not a day goes by without them thinking of the daughter they lost. Memories of Jeralee are everywhere in their home—photographs of a smiling Jeralee look out from almost every room. But nowhere are the reminders of their first-born daughter stronger than in the faces of their five remaining children, especially their three younger daughters. Today, just as Jeralee did, each of the children help with the daily household chores, with even the youngest daughter taking her turn at preparing the evening meal.

On a bright fall Saturday morning, following the death of his daughter, Jeff Underwood drove to Idaho Falls, to the banks of the Snake River where his daughter had died. In the back of his pickup he carried a "scarecrow" he had made. A photocopied picture of James Wood's face was taped to the head of the straw figure.

Jeff waited almost forty-five minutes, until a group of people fishing nearby had left. When he was alone, he placed the scarecrow near the big sagebrush where Jeralee was killed four months earlier. He took an ax, a shovel and pitchfork from his truck. For a moment, Jeff stared at the image of the man who had killed his child and mutilated her body. Then, he began to flail at the dummy with the ax, then the shovel and the pitchfork.

"At first, I thought it was the stupidest thing I'd ever done," Jeff said. "My counselor had recommended I do it. But as I began to hit at the scarecrow, I could feel some of the anger I had deep inside beginning to leave. I knew I had to get rid of the anger in a healing way, and this was how I should do it. I was taking my anger out on something that wouldn't be hurt."

Finally, exhausted, Jeff stopped. The scarecrow lay in shreds. He gathered the remains and threw them in the cold waters of the Snake River.

Since the death of their daughter, Jeff and Joyce Underwood have become advocates for victims' rights, and were instrumental in helping pass a victim's rights law in Idaho in 1995.

In September of 1994, Scott Shaw resigned from the Pocatello Police Department, and went to work as an investigator for the Idaho Attorney General's Office in Boise. In January of 1996 he accepted the position of police chief in nearby Preston, Idaho. The new job brought changes to Shaw's life. And, there were other changes as well. Although he had been raised a Mormon, he had not been active in the church until the September following Jeralee's death. He had begun to think about church as he attended prayer services of Jeralee at the LDS Stake Center in Pocatello. He was moved by the outpouring of compassion by the hundreds of people who had attended.

"I had been dealing with the bad side of life for so long," Shaw said, "But when I saw all those people, I was reminded that there are good people in the world afterall."

That Fall, his daughter had asked him to go with her to a Sacrament Service on her birthday. Shaw went, and has been active in the LDS church since.

The Wood case affected Shaw in other ways, too. Hunting deer and elk in the mountains had been a passion of Shaw's since childhood. But his hunting came to a stop after the summer of 1993. "I haven't been able to hunt since. I just don't have it in me to kill anything."

Shaw's investigation of Wood eventually led to the clearance of more than forty sex crimes and 180 armed robberies.

Today, James Wood sits on death row at the Idaho State Penitentiary in Boise. As a death row inmate, he is isolated from the general prison population and is housed in a single cell, seven by fourteen feet. He spends twenty-three hours a day in lockdown, and is allowed to go outside one hour a day. He passes time doing artwork—pencil and char-coal sketches.

Acknowledgments

This true story could not have been written without the openness and help of a great many people, especially those in Pocatello whose lives were changed by the events that are described here. Thanks to Scott Shaw for inviting me to work on this project, and special thanks to Jeff and Joyce Underwood and their children for sharing with me an enormously painful part of their lives. Their kindness and faith is an inspiration. They are indeed special people.

I also wish to thank Jan Anderson and Mark Hiedeman whose hospitality and assistance I greatly appreciated. I am also indebted to Dave Haggard, Liz Smith, Tammy Retzloff, and many others who were willing to be interviewed for this book. Special thanks also to Gene and Pauline Davis and Cindy Mancini. Finally, I am grateful for the support from my late father, Clyde R. Adams, and mother, Mozelle Adams, and especially my wife, Cary. Her help and encouragement meant the world to me, and always will.

Terry Adams

I wish to thank my brothers and sisters for their consistent and enthusiastic encouragement. I'm obliged to my colleague and friend, Scott Shaw, for his impeccable partnership in our ongoing research on James Wood.

I also thank my forensic peers at the American College of Forensic Examiners and the Hardiman Task Force for their support. Also, I want to thank Rod Colvin, of Addicus Books, for the opportunity he has afforded to all of us.

Lastly, I am beholden to my husband, who has been the perfect advocate, and who has always supported my professional endeavors.

Mary Brooks-Mueller

I would like to thank my family for their infinite patience and understanding. A special thanks to my parents, Frank and Doris Shaw and my brother Frank for his support; he has always been a shining example for me.

Scott Shaw

About the Authors

Terry Adams graduated from Auburn University, Auburn, Alabama, with a bachelor of fine arts degree in 1969. He began his writing career as an advertising copywriter in Atlanta, Georgia. Today he is working on a novel, and is a regular contributor to the Review & Comment section of *The Birmingham News*. Adams, his wife, Cary, and their cocker spaniel, Penny, live in the San Francisco Bay area.

Mary Brooks-Mueller, Ph.D. is a board certified forensic examiner and the managing partner of Forensic Consultants LLP in Montana. Her professional interests include forensic consultation, psychobiographical research, and document analysis. Brooks-Mueller earned her doctorate in clinical psychology from the Fielding Institute, Santa Barbara, California, in 1997. From 1977 to 1990, she served as a clinical sciences instructor at several colleges and universities in the Midwest. She and her husband live in Montana.

Scott Shaw is the Chief of Police in Preston, Idaho. Prior to accepting his current position, he served with the police force in Pocatello, Idaho, for seventeen years, from 1977 to 1994. Shaw has two decades experience in criminal profiling and interrogation techniques; he developed the Investigative Protocol for Sex Offense Investigations, currently used by numerous police departments.

Scott and his wife make their home in Idaho. They have three sons and a daughter.

Addicus Books

Visit the Addicus Books Web Site
http://members.aol.com/addicusbks

Eye of the Beast $16.95
  T. Adams, M. Brooks-Mueller, S. Shaw
  ISBN 1-886039-32-1

The Street-Smart Entrepreneur
133 Tough Lessons I Learned the Hard Way $14.95
  Jay Goltz, ISBN 1-886039-33-X

The Healing Touch — Keeping the Doctor/
Patient Relationship Alive Under Managed Care $9.95
  David Cram, MD ISBN 1-886039-31-3

Hello, Methuselah! Living to 100 and Beyond $14.95
  George Webster ISBN 1-886039-259

The Family Compatibility Test $9.95
  Susan Adams ISBN 1-886039-27-5

First Impressions — Tips to Enhance Your Image $14.95
  Joni Craighead ISBN 1-886039-26-7

Straight Talk About Breast Cancer $9.95
  Susan Braddock, MD ISBN 1-886039-21-6

Prescription Drug Abuse — The Hidden Epidemic $14.95
  Rod Colvin ISBN 1-886030-22-4

The ABCs of Gold Investing $14.95
  Michael J. Kosares ISBN 1-886039-29-1

The Flat Tax: Why It Won't Work for America $12.95
  Scott E. Hicko ISBN 1-886039-28-3

Suddenly Gone $15.95
  Dan Mintrione ISBN 1-886039-23-2

Counterpoint - A Murder in Massachusetts Bay $16.95
  Margaret Press, Joan Noble Pinkham ISBN 1-886039-24-0

Please send:

_____ copies of _____

(Title of book)

at $ _____ each   TOTAL   _____

Nebr. residents add 5% sales tax   _____

Shipping/Handling
  $3.00 for first book.
  $1.00 for each additional book.   _____

TOTAL ENCLOSED   _____

Name_____

Address_____

City _____ State ___ Zip _____

☐ Visa ☐ Master Card ☐ Am. Express

Credit card number _____

Expiration date _____

Order by credit card, personal check or money order.
Send to:

Addicus Books
Mail Order Dept.
P.O. Box 45327
Omaha, NE 68145
Or, order **TOLL FREE: 800-352-2873**